Alan Oliver.

&

Brian Martin

Rutland

Landscapes and Legends

Text by Brian Martin
Paintings by Alan Oliver

Cottage
Publications

First published by Cottage Publications,
an imprint of Laurel Cottage Ltd.
Donaghadee, N. Ireland 2008.
Copyrights Reserved.
© Illustrations by Alan Oliver 2008.
© Text by Brian Martin 2008.
All rights reserved.
No part of this book may be reproduced or stored on any media
without the express written permission of the publishers.
Design & origination in Northern Ireland.
Printed & bound in China.
ISBN 978 1 900935 70 8

The Author

Brian Martin was born in Nottingham in 1941 and worked as an advertising copywriter in London before joining the Leicester Mercury group as a feature writer.

He retired from full-time journalism in January 2008 after 40 years in newspapers and magazines. He was deputy editor at both the *Grantham Journal* and *Newark Advertiser* and edited the *Rutland Times.* His last job was with the Stamford Mercury where he wrote the weekly Life Of Brian column for three years. He lives in Cottesmore.

The Artist

Alan Oliver is recognised as one of the Midlands' leading landscape artists. Aged 70, he was born in Southampton though his family moved to Stamford when he was three. Alan's first job was as an apprentice engineer with Baker Perkins in Peterborough.

He later became a graphic designer and technical illustrator before working as a film animator and eventually becoming a professional artist. His distinctive work has popularised the beauty of Rutland far beyond its boundaries and he is in great demand for commissions and exhibitions. He lives in Oakham.

Contents

Rutland – Past, Present and Future

I once interviewed a nice old chap who had auditioned for the Halle Orchestra during the war, when all the young men were away. An amateur cellist, he was asked to play a snatch of melody on his instrument.

The Halle's conductor Sir John Barbirolli, himself a cellist, winced at his first attempts and gently re-positioned the man's stubby fingers at the top of the strings. "Blimey, I ain't never been up there before!" exclaimed the old boy.

It's much the same with Rutland. Many folk "ain't been up here before." They should try it.

Multum in Parvo. Much In Little. The legend on the county coat of arms – which comes complete with horseshoe pointing downwards for good luck – sums up England's smallest enclave in three words.

Population 34,000. Area 18 miles by 18 miles; 41 villages, each with its own unique identity. Two market towns. Say no more. The figures are all there – but they don't tell the full story.

Rutland is an anachronism. Such rolling rural beauty shouldn't have a place in today's hard-nosed Britain. But, like a travelogue with its heart in the right place, Rutlanders talk proudly to envious outsiders of its glories.

Winding lanes, thatched cottages and sturdy Georgian manor houses are incorporated in an impossibly Elysian landscape and it's not true to say there are no *real* Rutlanders left – some of 'em can trace their roots back to Domesday.

True, those 'old boys' are being gradually outnumbered by outsiders but both share the same experience – to wake up each morning, rain or shine, and bless the day they chose to live in Rutland.

Newcomers rightly view their chosen terrain as a stress-free retreat – it would be, if it wasn't for the council tax – and Rutland is like pulling into the lay-by of life. Some people moan – shame on them – but most are happy to owe fealty to an ancient county which prides its independence as never before.

The name of Rutland has become something of a smart brand label. A certain Duke, whose castle lies just up the road in Belvoir, also carries its name with dignity – though some puzzled Americans wonder why he doesn't actually live here. It's too complicated to explain.

There are drawbacks. Flanked by the frantic A1 motorway – where commuters' coronaries come with each pint of petrol – Rutland sometimes seems to be as smug as an Ealing comedy, patting itself on its back with rampant glee at its own good fortune. Yet it's had to fight for survival.

The War of Independence is still fresh in our minds. Victory brought in an apolitical county council – since politicised after a fashion – which boasted more wing-commanders, squadron leaders and general good eggs than you'd find in a Gilbert and Sullivan songfest.

At least their hearts were in the right place. They curbed housing development beyond a certain height and restricted building to brownfield sites – of which, apparently, there were few.

Divorced from 'big brother' Leicestershire on April Fool's Day 1997 they exercised benign control and, for a time, gave the impression that all Whitehall pen pushers were irritants. Then, sadly, the truth sank in and Rutland had to compete hard and fast for Government cash. Cue for a change of tack.

The county's golden acres run from Thistleton in the north, to Cold Overton in the west, to Great Casterton in the east and to Caldecott in the south. Like a landlocked island of its own making, it has its own unique qualities. It's amiable but not too riotous, respectful but not servile, honest but not po-faced. But how did it all start?

The old area corresponding to Rutland was developed on the edge of the Fens, with the Welland Valley marking its southern boundary, and there was a 1,000-year history of separate continuity until the unseemly kerfuffle in 1974 that forced it into Leicestershire's arms.

It first arrived as an independent county rather late, in the 13th century, but it was part of a Roman estate in its infancy and became part of the dower of the Queens of Mercia, and then the Queens of England. Its special position on the frontier between Danes and English on the fringe of the Leighfield Forest – together with its proximity to the Great North Road – emphasised its importance as a last bastion of pre-Conquest England. Its evolution has emphasised the strength of historical continuity.

Saxton's first known map of the county in 1576 shows it with forests ringed round and various fanciful humps and clumps scattered at random around Cotesmore, Okeham and Uppyghm (sic). It does not, however, show the capacity for industry, and visitors to the excellent Rutland Railway Museum – one of the county's many tourist attractions – will be surprised to learn of the upheavals caused by centuries of quarrying.

There were once three separate ironstone sites around Cottesmore, plus another one near Market Overton. Quarrying continues near Greetham and other parts of the county – particularly Ketton – and industrial expansion has always been at odds with the image of waving wheatfields and babbling brooks. But although the numbers of lorries that rumble daily through Rutland's narrow lanes have multiplied, the scars of industry remain well concealed. Holiday homeowners need have no fears.

Take Oakham. It remains a charming county town often compared unfairly with such TV puppet hotbeds as Trumpton and Chigley but in fact in touch with reality. Its town partnership of traders is advocating a new-look High Street with wider pavements, boulevard-style cafes and just one line of free-flowing traffic and light industry is hugging the bypass. Small 'cottage' businesses and computer firms proliferate around the area. Most folk would say Oakham's got it about right.

With its 1191 castle lined with horseshoes donated by the rich and famous, its cosy market place, its magnificent church of All Saints and its proximity to Rutland Water, it's a tourist trap for any visitor seeking to re-discover a Britain of sentimental memory – one that's largely ceased to exist in our major cities.

Major supermarkets are scattered about but a number of small shops remain. The sight of them is refreshing in an era when many town centres are beginning to look the same. With a population of 12,000, Oakham has more bijou quality stores – selling everything from antiques to chic West End fashions – than most places of its size. Its markets on Wednesdays and Saturdays attract traders from far afield and its farmers' market, promoting local produce – and why not? – has a popular spot on Gaol Street. And, like Uppingham, it has a great time around Christmas when the streets are transformed by twinkling lights, Santa holds court by the Buttercross and there's a right knees-up round the square.

Oakham also enjoys its fair share of greenery. Volunteers from the award-winning Oakham in Bloom group work prodigiously to ensure it's festooned with flowers throughout the summer months, giving it the look of a small spa town.

Cutts Close, behind All Saints church, offers a large area of grassland on which to flop after shopping. Bands play on its bandstand in a series of summer concerts sponsored by the town council and the carnival brings in merrymakers in droves.

A series of humps and hollows to the east of the Close reminds us that the Melton-Oakham canal once ended there. The heyday of the British canal network was at the turn of the 20th century but it remains a mistaken belief in 21st century society that waterways – along with rail branch lines – have no further part to play in a modern transport system. Thankfully stretches of the local canal are still accessible to enthusiasts – as are some of the pubs that once serviced them.

Pubs? Now we're talking. The Odd House Inn in Oakham, for instance, was once a regular venue for boatmen; now it's among a plethora of commendable pub/restaurants. Some superior eateries – like Nick's at the Lord Nelson in the Market Place – are tucked away cosily, adding an extra intimacy. Others are more spectacularly obvious.

Oakham market place provides a suitable starting point for bon viveurs. The Whipper-In hotel occupies a generous slice of one flank. Formerly called the George, it was once a busy watering hole for farmers, land agents and local characters like 'Scuttles' Burton who, with his pet dog, occupied pole position in the tap room. Whatever happened to Scuttles? Presumably such inoffensive old topers such as Mr Burton exited at speed when they saw the latest sorry batch of lager louts come galumphing over the horizon.

The Wheatsheaf, across the road from All Saints church, is a welcoming low-beamed haunt of sportsmen, off-duty teachers, shoppers and wayfaring intellectuals. Just up the road, the Railway – within tooting distance of the trains – is hung about with pot mugs bearing the insignias of every Football League club. Its landlord supports Leicester City but is otherwise a decent chap.

All real ale roads lead to the Grainstore. Housed in a huge former warehouse, it's well worth visiting – whether you're waiting for a train or just tired of trotting. Since Ruddles stopped making their beer at Langham, and Oakham Ales moved to Peterborough, the Grainstore has had the local commercial brewing business largely to itself.

More country inns have been converted to high class gastro pubs. Rutland has its fair share. The Olive Branch at Clipsham was once a rundown dogpat; now it's a Michelin-stars winner. The Exeter Arms at Barrowden is acclaimed for its food and home-brewed ale. The Old Plough at Braunston has a refectory, patio, beer garden and petanque court. The White Horse at Empingham is warm, friendly and strategically sited on the road to Stamford. But enough of my regular haunts.

Some people say Oakham lacks facilities. Not so. True, there is no fixed building for a cinema, though the Vale of Catmose College hosts regular film seasons. There is no fixed concert hall either, though the magnificent Victoria Hall stages concerts as does the Oakham School chapel and All Saints church. There is also no established community theatre, though the Queen Elizabeth Theatre, part of Oakham School, presents plays, often by the Rutland Arts Theatre Society – RATS to you.

No-one seems to actually *own* Oakham, especially not Tesco, which has a large store off South Street. It remains a rather quaint free spirit, tucked snugly into its valley like a cup in a saucer with Rutland Water close at hand and good walking and riding country all around. Some of the views are stupendous – one from the high hills overlooking Barleythorpe foreshortens the proximity of Oakham to Rutland Water and creates a scene that could have come straight from the Rhine.

In the town itself, Oakham School continues to pursue its laudable commitment as a co-ed academy. It produces some of the brightest pupils in the land, with a record number of Duke of Edinburgh awards, and though its quadrangled heart is in the centre of Oakham, its boarding houses, labs and studios extend along the Ashwell Road. It has a fine reputation for sport and its playing fields are scattered beyond that same blessed bypass which has helped the town cope so swiftly with congestion.

Oakham School has brought considerable kudos to the town. Former pupils include D H Everett, who commanded HMS Ajax at the Battle of the River Plate, William Dodd, chaplain to George III, and John Cope, former Paymaster General.

Similarly with Uppingham School. The alma mater of such diverse figures as Donald Campbell, Boris Karloff, Rick Stein, Stephen Fry and England cricketer Percy Chapman, it offers yet another splendid edifice, which dominates its surroundings like an Oxbridge college. Pleasantly perched on its ridge,

Uppingham sometimes seems like a Barsetshire enclave with no relevance to the Space Age. Which is all to its credit.

The eternal joy of Rutland in general is in its capacity to surprise and delight. Its villages are often well within cycling distance and anybody hiring a bike from Rutland Water can pedal peaceful tree-shaded roads that lope through pastoral acres which look largely untouched by history.

The past, of course, was a different matter. Graveyards show evidence of whole generations dying in a single hamlet. Many might never have left it for the day but, with gracious hindsight, we have to thank them for being custodians of a land we now enjoy.

We can hardly imagine how hard they must have worked. A year's wages 380 years ago would buy less than a litre of petrol today. A male servant who could make a hayrick and kill a pig – though, presumably, not at the same time – could get 50 shillings a year. But they weren't thinking of the scenery when they tilled the land; they were just hooked on survival.

So much for then, when communities were rigorously respectful, insular and bounded by nature's parameters. Now every 'secret' place in Britain is easily accessible – and every conceivable form of transport known to man is pressed into service to pollute the atmosphere whilst taking in the view.

In a way it's a blessing. How else would people from smoke-grimed towns have learned about the glories of Lyddington Bede House, the panoramic brushstroke sweeps of landscape between, say, Market Overton and Whissendine and the solid splendour of the magnificent railway viaduct stretching across the vale near Seaton?

Other delights await. Yew Tree Avenue, just beyond Clipsham on the road to Castle Bytham, is one of the most beautiful sites in all Britain with trees topiarised into everything from aeroplanes to unicorns bordering a wide grassy pathway that stretches into the distance towards Clipsham Hall.

Exton is a picturebook village with a handsome green. Part of the Exton estate, its almost perennial peace is disturbed just once a year – when a mammoth street market at the end of May snakes its way through the lanes and barns, and parked cars pack Lord Gainsborough's fields. The rain may sluice down – as it has in recent years – but Exton remains defiant. The jazz band plays, the village hall serves scones, the elders play tombola and all's well with the world.

Similarly at Braunston, on the other side of the county, where its Happening is a feast of Olde England, compete with maypole dancing, madrigal singers and the crowning of the May Queen. Like Extonians, Braunstonians are also weatherproof. Everyone retreats to the village hall if wet.

Teigh, beyond Market Overton in the north-west of the county, is a tiny gem of calm with a handsome church – unusually with lengthway pews – and few distractions. Like many another estate village, Teigh has no pub. Greetham, on the other hand, currently has three – for better or worse – and its buildings include the extraordinary home of Victorian stonemason William Halliday who apparently helped himself to surplus stone fragments whilst repairing local churches and thus created a house containing a curious mix of remnants, including whole sections of 13th and 14th century windows. It's an eyecatcher for anyone who either negotiates the narrow main street – with many of its buildings smack up to the roadway – or heads for one of those aforementioned three pubs.

History really is all around. You just have to find it. For example, the dastardly Gunpowder Plot was allegedly hatched in a room in the spire of Stoke Dry church and the outline of a Roman fort can be traced at Great Casterton. The tiny church of St Peter's, Brooke was praised by the poet John Betjeman, while Fort Henry – which is only accessible on rare occasions

– was once *the* place to party for the cocktail classes. Set back amidst trees on the lane between Exton and the A1, it overlooks a patch of water on which mock naval battles were staged. One can imagine the chink of glasses and up-tempo rhythms of Roy Fox on the record player.

Archaeologists digging in the Hambleton valley, before it was flooded to create Rutland Water, unearthed Iron Age, Roman and Anglo Saxon remains and artefacts. Some of their finds are on display at the former Normanton church with its Georgian upper walls and spire elevated above the lapping waters of the busy reservoir.

So there's nothing new about Rutland but it remains a very special place. Let's hope it's left in peace for others to enjoy.

Many homes were submerged when Rutland Water was created. One couple whose cottage was 'drowned' when their valley was flooded were one of the first to take a boat trip across the reservoir soon after it was opened in 1977.

The wife recalled: "We'd travelled for about ten minutes when my husband, who was rowing, asked me to look down into the water. When I asked him: 'What am I supposed to be looking at?' he answered: 'Our house; it's right beneath you'. I felt absolutely devastated."

There was originally much opposition to the scheme. Posters of protest were pasted everywhere and many Rutlanders feared their beloved county would become 'a towpath round a lake.'

Happily that hasn't happened and there's still plenty of little Rutland left for the wicked developers to have a go at. Yet settlements on sites dating back to Anglo-Saxon times were duly swamped and deprived residents were rehoused, though some claimed they received scant compensation. An elevated village was left to represent the Hambletons on its promontory.

Rutland Water was devised by Anglian Water as one of the biggest man-made lakes in Western Europe, larger even than the naturally evolved Windermere in the Lake District. It was carved out of the soil to meet the increasing demands of such expanding places as Northampton, Kettering and Peterborough and cost £29m to construct. It was 8km long and had a 39km perimeter, a water volume of 124m cubic metres and a water surface of 1,260 hectares.

But despite the qualms, it soon attracted shoals of visitors. The influx – particularly from Leicester – boosted the local economy, with at least 13,000 people visiting the site on a single Sunday in 1977. Millions have used it since.

Attractions include sailing, angling and water sports. Keep-fit enthusiasts flock to hire bikes, run the round-reservoir track and climb the Rokblok. Children enjoy the adventure playground, wonder at the butterfly farm and troop to Normanton church, which in a minor miracle of engineering, was raised above water level to be used as a museum. A bird watching and wildlife centre sited at nearby Egleton has won international acclaim.

Development around the basin has been largely controlled. The effect on the villages around its rim has been largely beneficial and tourism has boosted Rutland's coffers. "Don't Flood Rutland!" the locals cried all those years ago. Many have changed their tune since.

Rutland Water

NORMANTON CHURCH

Composer Edward German's stirring ditty *The Yeomen of England* could have been written about my old friend Ray Hill who lives, breathes and – as far as I know – sleeps Burley.

The amiable Ray comes from several generations of farm tenants who all owed allegiance to the owners of Burley-on-the-Hill, a grand mansion standing proud on a 500ft scarp.

The gracious house is forefronted by cottages – set at a respectful distance off the same Oakham-Cottesmore highway once traversed by Cromwell's cavalry.

Glorious meadows slope to the Stamford road and the former smithy on Burley green inspired Longfellow to write his famous poem about The Village Blacksmith as well as becoming a famous trademark for Cherry Blossom boot polish.

Ulf the Saxon – who sounds commendably butch – built the first residence, a castle, 200 yards from the present mansion on a ridge. Later landowners included members of the Finch and Harrington families. One of the latter was almost bankrupt by New Year festivities in 1595 when Mr Shakespeare's company of actors was summoned express from London to perform *Titus Andronicus* – not most people's first choice for a lively party.

The 1st Duke of Buckingham, a Royal favourite, then bought Burley as a hunting lodge, but his son the 2nd Duke fled during the English Civil War, leaving the house, apart from the stables, to be gutted by Parliamentarians. It was rebuilt by Daniel Finch, 2nd Earl of Nottingham in the early 18th century but – guess what – was again swept by fire on August 9, 1908. A certain Mr Winston Churchill – a guest at a house party the previous night – distinguished himself during the blaze by trying to help the Oakham fire brigade fight the flames but, according to one observer, 'kept getting in the way.' One hopes his cigar hadn't started it.

The refurbished house was used as an officers' convalescent hospital during both world wars and as a post-war sanatorium before reverting to the ownership of Col James Hanbury.

The loquacious Raymond Hill – himself no mean local historian – thought his beloved Burley would be lost forever when Polly Peck tycoon Asdil Nadir devised a five-star hotel with adjacent golf courses. Fortunately architect and developer Kit Martin seized the opportunity to convert the stately mansion into 32 luxury properties. The building retains its Georgian grandeur as a magnificent backdrop to the annual Rutland County Show and the rest, as they say, is history.

Burley

BURLEY-ON-THE-HILL

A sunny Sunday in peaceful Brooke, in the distance a cock crows and there's the delicious smell of cooking from a nearby cottage.

The hush is complete but it wasn't always as quiet as this. Brooke was once prided for its medieval Augustinian priory, complete with feisty prior. Now its remains lie in humps and bumps near Brooke Priory House, former home of the Noel family.

Delightful Brooke has long relied on its exquisite church of St Peter's for worship. Originally 12th century, much of it was rebuilt in 1579 – one of the very few churches to be enhanced post-Reformation.

Elizabethan features include square-headed windows and box pews, some of them marked with ancient graffiti. A marble effigy commemorates Charles, son of Andrew Noel, who died in 1619 aged 28. Memorial slabs set into the stone floor mark the last resting places of members of the 18th century Rawllins family and the church also boasts framed facsimile copies of pages from the 1559 Book of Common Prayer and the 1611 'Judas' Bible - in which, in one section, a dozy printer substituted the traitor's name for that of Jesus. Quelle horreur!

A 13th century reliquary box, a casket made to hold religious relics, was unearthed on the site of the former monastery in 1805 and now resides in Rutland County Museum. Little Brooke is a joy, tucked away in the folds above the Gwash.

Further downstream, Braunston is famous for its Happening, a joyous Maytime knees-up harking back to days of yore. Maypole dancing is perennially organised by the splendid Mrs Sylvia Matthews, who also happens to be a champion blood donor, while a soccer tournament is organised by Sylvia's sterling husband Paul.

The local girl who is chosen as Queen of the Happening leads a parade through the streets and everyone has a jolly time at the village's two pubs.

The church clock, unusually, sits outside its tower and although the old village has experienced much infilling it remains a charming settlement.

Its villagers were once known as 'Braunston Turks' for their ferocity – one of their number used to win bets by biting live rats to death – but they're friendly enough these days.

Brooke

BROOKE TO BRAUNSTON

Alan Oliver. 08

Oakham, Rutland's compact county town, originally fringed the Royal forest of Leighfield and was granted by William the Conqueror to his blacksmith Walkelin de Ferrers. The latter's legacy lives on in the stone-flagged castle which is dominated by hung horseshoes of all sizes dating back more than 500 years.

Most were donated by passing Royalty and gentry as a 'forfeit' for safe passage. King Edward IV presented the first after the nearby Battle of Loosecoat Field and the most recent ones were given on behalf of the Queen, the Prince of Wales and the Princess Royal.

Oakham's impressive parish church is All Saints, just off the market place, with a fine spire erected with money left by local benefactor Roger Flore. A passageway alongside leads to Cutts Close, a large grassy area whose humps and bumps mark the former terminus of the Melton-Oakham canal. It's a regular venue for the Cottesmore Hunt's Boxing Day meet and comes into its own on Carnival Sunday. A nearby pub called The Odd House is one of Oakham's oldest.

The town's quaint market place is tucked away off the High Street and surrounded by old buildings. It features a Buttercross and a set of stocks with an odd number of holes – leading to speculation that at least part of it was built for a either a one-legged villain or a very small boy!

Public whippings were held there until the late 18th century, with celebrated 'rogue and vagabond' John Smith being flogged on successive Saturdays – not so much Match of the Day as Lash of the Day – while another unfortunate, a woman, was whipped for stealing wood.

The partly-cobbled square, with its Georgian and Victorian buildings, has been used for filming, with *Nicholas Nickleby* featuring several local 'extras' dressed in period attire and 'rhubarbing' briskly in the background. It stands adjacent to Oakham School, founded by the ubiquitous Archdeacon Johnson.

The school's original 16th century building stands behind the church but today's academic hub is concentrated on a quadrangle west of the market place with state-of-the-art boarding houses and teaching labs spread elsewhere. The school has an excellent headmaster in the soccer-mad Joe Spence and its cricket ground is in great demand for Leicestershire one-day matches. Summer speech days are also held there – in a marquee on the lawn – but much depends on the weather.

Oakham

THE BUTTER CROSS

Alan Olivier.

Oakham's western flank once featured alleys of cramped cottages. A giant Tesco now stands where, until recently, there was a farm, but at least one historic building remains nearby – the tiny chapel of St John and St Anne, erected during the reign of Richard the Lionheart and beautifully restored 20 years ago. Now it forms the centrepiece of a block of flats for the elderly.

There's some history, too, at the level crossing where the signal box was once used as a model for Hornby train sets. And also making history is the award-winning Grainstore brewery, which offers tours for all those who want to see the brewing process from start to finish. The sweet scent of malt and hops regularly permeates the town.

A newly built bypass has thankfully removed extraneous traffic from Oakham centre, but juggernauts continue to rumble within feet of a charming thatched cottage on the Melton Road. The birthplace of the 17th century belligerent midget Jeffrey Hudson, it attracts scores of tourists each year.

Oakham Castle

Victoria Hall, a well-known town meeting place, is another familiar landmark, but most Oakhamians reckon the proudest survivor of the past is the ancient Flores House which extended into the main thoroughfare until 1914, leaving just the narrowest of passing points for vehicles. Dating from the 13th century, it was the medieval home of illustrious wool merchant, local benefactor and one-time Speaker of the House of Commons Roger Flore who was a great patron of All Saints church.

A brisk walk east of the Burley Road/Mill Street junction (an ancient crossroads) takes in the smart, low-level library to the left and the illustrious Rutland County Museum – formerly an indoor riding academy – to the right. Rutland's administrative offices are a little further on at Catmose, once a handsome family mansion set in parkland and still retaining some of its spoilt grandeur, but there are grim reminders ahead.

A gibbet once stood on the old Uppingham road by a bridge and local miscreants were hung there as a form of spectator sport. It must have been a miserable journey from the assizes (held at the castle) to the gaol to the gibbet. No wonder so many fainted within sight of the gallows. Hence Swooning Bridge. The gibbet's long gone but the name remains.

Oakham

FLORES HOUSE

Residents of Cresswell Drive, Cottesmore might guess at their road being linked with watercress. They could be right, too, as the cress beds along Mill Lane were once reckoned the best in the county.

Cottesmore was originally Cott's Moor. Flocks were washed in the Sheepdyke and villagers would carry their pots and pans down a little lane to the dyke to wash their utensils. Hence Clatterpot Lane.

The Clipsham stone spire of St Nicholas' church can be seen from miles around and the building's mainly 14th century interior includes an RAF chapel to emphasise its connections with the nearby airbase. The pleasant church was once linked with plough pioneer Richard Baker and scholar Peter Gunning whose work was mentioned in the diaries of both Samuel Pepys and John Evelyn. A sad plaque on the war memorial mourns rector's son Geoffrey Ellwood, one of the many to have perished young on the Western Front during the First World War.

The thatched Sun Inn is a welcoming hostelry which, until recently, held jolly Christmas 'bucket drinking parties' for which participants were awarded commemorative ties.

The Cottesmore Hunt's former kennels stand empty alongside the Easson garage. The pack long ago transferred to the Ashwell road, not far from the Rutland Railway Museum, a steam loco lover's Shangri-la which does a roaring trade at bank holidays.

Traffic rumbles through Cottesmore on its way to the A1 from Oakham – as it does through Greetham just a mile down the road. The discovery of a Romano-British kiln in a nearby quarry suggests the latter was an important Anglo Saxon site whose narrow main street may once have gone closer to St Mary's church than the current road. Dickersons' quarry lies just up the road.

A stream runs through the village and it has three pubs – a remarkable number for such a small village, though it prides itself on its strong community spirit.

Barrow hamlet is out on a loop on the Market Overton road. There is only one way in by car and a gnarled notice painted in 19th century script warns: *'All vagrants who are found begging in this town will be taken up and prosecuted.'*

At one time Barrow had a tavern and a chapel. Now it's an isolated, peaceful backwater with the remnants of a market cross at its heart.

Cottesmore

BEST CRESSED

Two of Rutland's proudest assets are RAF Cottesmore and the Cottesmore Hunt. The latter now operates from its new kennels off the Ashwell road while the airfield is just out of the main village, yet both remain essential parts of the Cottesmore community and the vacated stone buildings of the former hunt HQ still stand at the corner of Mill Lane and Main Street.

Origins of the Cottesmore Hunt go back more than 300 years when a pack of foxhounds from Westmoreland was delivered to local landowner Henry, Viscount Lowther. The hunt was officially established in the late 18th century and still prides itself as a subscription pack, not dependant on aristocratic patronage but receiving support from a wide cross-section of the community. The latter has proved particularly vital in combating recent anti-hunt legislation.

The Cottesmore is considered a premier Shire pack – along with the neighbouring Quorn, Belvoir and Fernie – and attracts many overseas members, particularly from the United States. It works closely with reliant rural businesses and has enhanced much of the landscape over the years by planting 'fox copses' such as Prior's Coppice and Ranksborough Gorse, names familiar throughout the world of hunting.

There has been an airfield in Cottesmore since March 1938 when it was opened in anticipation of the forthcoming conflict in Europe. The very first squadrons flew Wellesleys but soon converted to the Fairey Battle, an excellent training aircraft which unfortunately lost out to the German Messerschmitts over France in the early months of the Second World War.

Bomber Command then took over the base, flying Handley Page Hampdens as part of 1,000-bomber raids over Germany in 1942. The base had been re-equipped with Wellington bombers and became a storage centre for Horsa gliders before American aircrews arrived in September 1943. At one time there were 3,700 US personnel on base, and members of the 505th Parachute Infantry Regiment took part in the D-Day landings in Normandy in June 1944.

Since the Americans left in May 1945, Cottesmore has maintained its frontline role – first as a V-Force base under war hero Group Capt 'Johnnie' Johnson, then as a tri-national training establishment with three Tornado squadrons before becoming a Harrier base in 2002. A Naval Strike Wing was formed as part of a Harrier Joint Force, and current plans envisage a new multi-role Joint Fighter Group within ten years.

Cottesmore

CUTTS CLOSE MEET

Alan Oliver

Historians claim Lyddington could have grown bigger than Uppingham – Rutland's 'second city' a few miles north – had it been sited nearer the main Rockingham road.

As it is, the only sign of a struggle for supremacy comes in the shape of an ancient market cross – one of the few reminders that 'Long Lyddington' was once close to being a township.

Yet an attractive straggle of mainly ironstone houses down a single wide thoroughfare still identifies Lyddington as one of Rutland's prettiest villages, drawing hundreds of visitors each year to admire St Andrew's church and marvel at the stately Bede House – the palatial dwelling of successive Bishops of Lincoln for almost 500 years.

There must have been quite a stir in medieval times when the bishop and his retinue arrived, with full panoply, for one of their regular stays. But in 1547 it all came to an abrupt halt when the building was seized on behalf of the church-bashing Henry VIII as part of his nationwide subjugation of the Roman Catholic Church.

The Bede House was first handed over to Lord Gregory Cromwell, a son of Henry's oleaginous aide Thomas Cromwell, before being passed on to the Cecils of Burghley who had it converted into almshouses in 1602.

The building is now administered by English Heritage and is open to the public. The Bishop's Eye, a stone structure like a mini-tower with an access passage like the eye of a needle, guards a corner of the precinct wall leading to the main house which contains, among other things, a magnificently carved 400-year-old ceiling, a series of splendid fireplaces and heraldic glass of the utmost quality.

St Andrew's stands next to the Bede House. Its friendly acoustics make it ideal for concert performances and the ever-rewarding Music in Lyddington series is based there, with many famous soloists enjoying the relaxing 'gig' as a healthy antidote to busy schedules in London and abroad.

The church contains the fine brasses of Heleyn Hardy (1486) and Edward Watson (1530). It also includes an impressive window dedicated to 19th century parishioners John and Elizabeth Clarke and, somewhat mysteriously, stained glass featuring the image of a red-haired man.

Lyddington

THE BEDE HOUSE AND CHURCH

It's hard to believe the Olive Branch pub at Clipsham was once threatened with closure. A regular watering hole for 150 years, it seemed its last bell was about to be rung early in the millennium when a planning application threatened to revert it to private property.

But, to drinkers' delight, scores of locals fought a rearguard battle to save it. Thanks to an inspirational young team, it continues to attract a loyal clientele and win awards for its food.

The Clipsham area is famous for its prime building stone. Its illustrious inhabitants have included the amiable Russian-bred local historian Prince Galitzin and the Davenport-Handleys at Clipsham Hall among its residents.

Most folk are obviously proud of the Olive Branch success story yet, sadly, it's a rare triumph at a time when scores of rural pubs are closing nationwide. The strangely-named Jackson Stops – just a mile from Clipsham in leafy Stretton – is also fighting back against the Government's absurd drinking laws and constantly rising overheads by creating ever more attractive menus to pull in the punters.

The latter hostelry's unusual name was derived from a Mr H Jackson-Stops, who purchased the Stretton estate in 1940. It was formerly called the White Horse, the standing joke being that the Jackson Stops estate agents' sign was outside for so long that visitors though it was the pub's name. Well, now it is.

During the Second World War it was popular with stressed-out bomber crews from Cottesmore or Woolfox who chalked their names on a timbered beam in the barn bar while playing the old English game of nurdling.

A third interesting hostelry in the locality is the Ram Jam, formerly a coaching inn on the A1 and now a leading meeting place for businessmen heading north. Again there's a quaint title – said to be derived from a cheeky traveller instructing a gullible landlady to 'ram' one thumb in one hole in a barrel and 'jam' the other thumb in another to get both mild and bitter beer from the same cask. Whilst she was desperately trying to stem the flow, he drove off without paying.

Incidentally, a nearby landmark is Stocken Hall, whose stables were once famed as the birthplace of the Duke of Wellington's horse Copenhagen, an equine hero of the Battle of Waterloo. A prison is now based on the estate and ghosts are rumoured to populate the area.

Stretton and Clipsham

THE JACKSON STOPS

Alan Oliver

One of the best known works by the composer Frederick Delius is *The Walk To The Paradise Garden* picturing a young couple strolling hand-in-hand towards a hazy infinity.

Drive one mile east of Clipsham and you encounter Yew Tree Avenue – tucked away on the Lincolnshire border and arguably one of the smallest county's best-kept secrets.

Shafts of summer brilliance filter through the two lines of 150 manicured yews – some of them 200 years old – and segment the mown grass like moonbeams through a ballroom window. That's when the gentle hum of nature is at its height, with tortoiseshell butterflies lingering longingly above common spotted orchids and woodpeckers drilling in nearby woods.

The wide grassy path between regimented ranks of sculptured trees stretches half-a-mile to the boundary of Clipsham Hall in the misty distance. One fully expects to encounter heaven at that point, not the occasional muntjak. *'Rarely, rarely, comest thou, spirit of delight,'* wrote Shelley, and beautiful Yew Tree Avenue is as good as it gets.

It all started in 1870 when head forester Amos Alexander began shaping yews near the gatehouse as a hobby. The local squire was so impressed he asked Amos to cut topiary figures flanking either side of his carriage drive. The old boy was happy to oblige, and his son Charles and local villagers continued with the tradition until the Forestry Commission took over.

The trees are now skilfully clipped each September with designs including an anchor, a windmill, three bears, a deer, an elephant and an even a chair where visitors can take their ease. Specific allusions are made to the Spitfire, the Coronation and the Moon landing.

Yew Tree Avenue provides an ethereal experience in which time is suspended and, briefly, the world becomes a wonderland. Long may it thrive.

Yewtree Avenue

WHERE SHAPED TREES STAND LIKE SENTRIES

Alan Oliver. 08

Uppingham began life as a ridge top settlement. For centuries it offered a safe through route to drovers and traders high above the marshy downlands and its High Street became so long and straggly that it had to be split East and West for convenience.

A rash of little lanes and alleyways still runs from it – many incorporating antique shops and craft industries – and the town's original medieval grid can easily be recognised, with some of its stone buildings dating back to Tudor times.

Its pleasant Market Place is almost totally enclosed, with the Falcon Hotel, a former coaching inn; the Vaults, a low-ceilinged pub; an ironmonger's shop with an elevated plough advertising its wares; and, of course, the church of St Peter and St Paul with its 14th century tower, big-angled buttresses and tall, recessed spire. Jeremy Taylor, chaplain to the ill-fated King Charles I, was rector here from 1637-42.

The square is normally occupied by a plethora of parked cars but

Uppingham School

it comes alive for the annual fatstock show – the only one in England to be held in its traditional setting – and the town's Christmas festivities when the streets swirl with shoppers and Uppingham becomes Dickensian for the day.

Uppingham School is the town's pride and joy, growing with the centuries to become one of Britain's leading independent co-educational seats of learning. It all started with the Old School of 1584, still sited behind the church near the steep Scale Hill – a road that struggling stagecoaches tended to avoid in favour of gentler Queen Street – but the main school's facade has the appearance of a major Oxbridge college.

Its towering grandeur owes much to Victorian architect Sir Thomas Jackson, and a stone figure of Archdeacon Johnson – who founded both Oakham and Uppingham schools – can be seen holding a miniature representation of the very first building. A memorial also pays homage to inspirational 19th century headmaster Edward Thring, who sounds like a Goon Show character but in real life brooked no nonsense.

Uppingham remains a quintessential market town surrounded by lush farming country. Warwick Metcalfe, a fine cartographer and artist and one of its most distinguished residents, has captured much of its allure in a series of pictures featuring most of its town centre buildings in detail. Its western fringes lead to a precipitous plunge through a heavenly landscape en route to Market Harborough which is itself worth a visit. Eastwards lies Peterborough.

Uppingham

OF SCHOLARS AND STONES

Alan Oliver.

If Rutland is one of England's best-kept secrets, Lyndon is one of the county's most delightfully hidden gems.

I only discovered it recently – turning off the road that circumnavigates Rutland Water to find myself driving down a dipping, leafy lane that promised great enchantment at its end.

Long-established Rutlanders will, of course, huff and puff knowledgably about newcomers like me (only 10 years here and counting) being hitherto unaware of the glories of this slumbering settlement tucked away between the Manton-Edith Weston road and North Luffenham. But, hey, you discover something new every day and, to me, Lyndon was a revelation.

Village wakes are not much part of rural life these days but we know sleepy Lyndon had one. It offered a spectacular opportunity to the locals to let themselves go for a few precious hours – though some wakes staggered on for a week and it took some time to shake off the drunken influx of assorted intinerant traders, musicians, showmen and other outside influences.

Lyndon's wake was somewhat later than most – being the first Sunday after November 11th – but it still must have offered splendid jollifications after a hard year of pastoral toil. One can imagine sober reflection at St Martin's church mixed with hearty celebrations at nearby Lyndon Hall, which was once the home of Thomas Barker (1722-1809), later to be hailed worldwide as a pioneer of meteorology.

Squire Barker came from distinguished stock. His esteemed grandfather was the remarkable mathematician William Whiston – who was equally long-lived, dying at 85 and being buried in Lyndon churchyard – while his brother-in-law was the famous naturalist Gilbert White of Selbourne, Hampshire.

The two entrances to the church are still well defined – one via a walkway from the grand hall for the toffs and the other a humbler, upward path from the village for the plebs. A neglected building, which stands beyond the church, is also worth inspection. It was once the rectory and a short traverse through long grass, across what once must have been a walled orchard, reveals evidences of mullioned windows and ancient brickwork topped by tall chimneys. It must have been a fine house in its heyday. Now it stands, forlorn, like the Haversham home in *Great Expectations.*

Lyndon

LOST LANES AND HIDDEN SECRETS

Alan Olver

No apologies for the chapter heading. It comes from Tony Cutting's excellent millennium book on Bisbrooke. Intrigued? You should be; and it's worth risking a few Cutting remarks to plagiarise it.

First, the strawberries. Bisbrooke, a settlement on a scarp of around 400 souls, stands a-sprawling in splendid isolation between Lyddington and Uppingham and the whole village once combined to harvest fruit from burgeoning bowers. Once it was cherries and gooseberries; then it was strawberries, transported to Leicester and adjacent towns to be sold but also stockpiled for a massive annual picnic on the village green at which bands played and people fell about.

Luscious fruit was also sold from The Gate pub, and thereby hangs a tale. At one time all new customers at the inn had their ties trimmed with scissors by enthusiastic bar staff to make them welcome – shear lunacy, one might say – though it's not recorded whether future TV stars Stephen Fry, Rick Stein and Johnny Vaughan had their cravats cropped for seeking sanctuary there whilst rascally pupils at Uppingham School.

Now for the turkeys – not the gobblers you might expect but used in this context as an epithet for pugnacious Bisbrookeans of the 19th century who at one time included navvies fresh from the Manton-Kettering railway line who were said to 'fight like turkey cocks.'

And finally the baboons, which were part of a menagerie kept by the Pinder family, a Bisbrooke clan steeped in circus showbiz. Their llamas once chased the Cottesmore hounds and the family also had a dog which played dead on the command of 'Bang!' But the undoubted star was Micky, the tricycling baboon, who regularly nicked milk from village doorsteps and on one occasion had to be dissuaded from getting on the school bus. What a cheeky monkey.

Bisbrooke

STRAWBERRIES, TURKEYS AND BABOONS

Alan Oliver. 08.

The old huntsman's cry 'Tantivy!' is said to be derived from 'San Tibba' – possibly a corruption of St Tibba who dwelt in Ryhall during the seventh century. Whatever its source, it makes an ideal analogy for county famous for its hunting.

There aren't many saints in Rutland – more sinners – but Tibba was apparently a good egg, though something of a wild child in her youth. The niece of the powerful King Penda of Mercia, she eschewed all luxuries to live in a hermitage in Ryhall where St John's church now stands. Tibba loved country sports and eventually became the patron saint of hunters and falconers. Her feast day is December 16 and both she and her cousin Eabbas, who lived with her at the hermitage, had holy wells named after them.

So much for the blessed Tibba – now for Ryhall itself. For an inland village – tucked into Rutland's south-east corner just three miles from Stamford – it too has watery connections. At one time it was just a few miles from the Wash and was frequently flooded. The swamp-like Fens were also too close for comfort and the ubiquitous River Gwash still divides the lowland village whose name originally meant 'a river bend where rye is grown.'

Much of the old part of Ryhall centres around a bijou square flanked by the local shop, the church and one of the village's two pubs – the other being near the bridge over the Gwash. The church contains a plethora of dog-tooth decorations and grotesques and was probably once attended by peasant poet John Clare who worked as a lime burner in the vicinity during the early 19th century.

Ryhall – along with Bisbrooke, Preston and Seaton – kept the ancient Plough Monday tradition going until the 1920s. At its height the ceremony appeared to have involved several local lads following a brass band and browbeating villagers until they handed over some money.

Ryhall

ON THE TRAIL OF ST TIBBA

Alan Oliver

Isaac Newton lived here – but only as a child. The famous 17th century scientist stayed many times at the Manor House, his grandmother's dwelling, though his family home was actually some 10 miles away up the Great North Road at Woolsthorpe Manor, which is where an apple allegedly fell on his head prompting him to ponder on the meaning of gravity.

For something of a backwater, Market Overton has a lively legacy. The village's enthusiastic fieldwalkers' group continues to find enough Roman and Anglo Saxon artefacts – including the remains of a Roman villa – to prove it was once a town of some substance.

Set on a scarp north-west of Cottesmore, 'Marko' enjoys attractive views across the Vale of Catmose. It hosted an important medieval market, and the church of Sts Peter & Paul features a sundial said to have been presented by Newton himself.

A glorious patchwork of fields surrounds the village, with numerous trails for ramblers, riders and dog walkers.

Feast days were always welcomed by local farmworkers, who were joined in the early 19th century by detachments of thirsty navvies working on the Melton-Oakham Canal. A busy wharf once stood on the road to Teigh.

Workers hired for ironstone quarrying and railway expansion later replaced the canal contingent at feast days and one semi-sober 19th century chronicler claimed there were so many people crowded outside the village pub *you couldn't put a single penny between 'em.'*

Today's casual visitors will note the village's comprehensive variety of handsome architecture – much of it Georgian. Its compact village green comes complete with stocks – not used in anger since 1838 – and the whole area comes alive during Feast Weekend and Scarecrow Festival, during which many an unwary motorist has been known to slow down swiftly when confronted with a highly lifelike traffic policeman made of straw!

Thistleton Gap, a few miles east, was the scene of a major prize-fight in 1811 in which the English heavyweight champion Tom Cribb defeated the self-proclaimed world champion the American Tom Molyneux watched by an estimated crowd of 15,000, many of them from London. The open-air bout was fought at a spot where three counties – Leicestershire, Lincolnshire and Rutland – met and, prizefighting being illegal, it was a simple matter to move the whole show to the next county if another set of lawmen arrived!

Market Overton

STOCKS AND SHEARS

I once met the man who had been the last baby to be born at Martinsthorpe. Then aged 78 and living at Empingham, he recalled: "At my birth the doctor jokingly told my mother 'This boy is creating history; I feel like adopting him!'"

The village of Martinsthorpe once stood on a ridge near the A6003 Oakham-Uppingham, linked to Manton and Brooke with magnificent views south to Preston and north to Burley. Just one isolated building remains.

One factor in its decline was the old Oakham road changing course. At one time it cut through Martinsthorpe and Gunthorpe en route to Oakham but was later altered to an easterly route via Manton before settling on its current switchback to Preston.

The main reasons why villages vanish seem to include plague, pillage, enclosures and pasturing – with landowners evicting people to make space for grazing. Creative landscaping was also contributory. In 1764 the rich squire of Normanton ejected his tenants and their families from their homes because they spoiled his view.

The former settlements of Horn and Hardwick were once both medieval communities near the Great North Road in eastern Rutland and, by rights, should have prospered. They were certainly set far enough back from the major highway to avoid being attacked by footpads. On the face of it, both stood a stronger chance of continuous existence than their near neighbours at Exton. Yet both have gone – along with at least 30 other Rutland villages – while Exton thrives in the midst of a rural estate based on Exton Hall, with a handsome ivy-clad pub, stately buildings, tall trees and cute rows of cottages that make a perfect backdrop for the popular annual street market.

In Hardwick's case, being sited close to the bloody battleground of Loosecoat Field (1470) might have been its undoing. Could it have been devastated in the aftermath? The fate of Horn, however, remains even more of a mystery. Just a few grassy indentations in the shadow of Horn House show it was once a fair-sized community with its own street system. But by the mid-15th century 'all was waste' and by 1649 only a shepherd lived there.

The demise of the village of Loodall north of Langham is equally puzzling, as is the erasure of Snelston, north of Caldecott, which was mentioned in the *Domesday Book*. A settlement also existed between Barrow and Market Overton in the north of the county. All are, sadly, long gone.

Martinsthorpe

LOST PASTURES AND MISSING HAMLETS

Teigh, with its E-shaped cluster of cottages and smart farms, seems to be in a permanent state of slumber. But strange – and violent – things have happened here. Oh yes.

First the good news. Isolated Teigh – pronounced 'Tee' – prides itself in being one of only a handful of 'thankful villages' to have welcomed home every one of its community who served, in whatever capacity, in the First World War.

A brass tablet in Holy Trinity church confirms the fact, giving thanks to God for the safe return of all 13 villagers who went to war, including two women – Mary Rate and Miriam Scott – and four members of the Tidd family.

Holy Trinity – originally 12th century but with mainly Georgian embellishments – contains two impressive and handsomely constructed rows of boxed pews which, unusually, face each other. Its interior was employed by a TV company a few years back to represent the Parliament of 1642 in an Open University documentary about the English Civil War and, for a few brief days, Teigh was a film set, invaded by camera crews, yards of snaking cable and actors in full Carolean fig shouting 'Zounds' and practising their swordplay.

Quaint buildings abound nearby. 'Tea Cosy Cottage' (alias Nethersetts) hugs the nearby Market Overton road while thatched-turreted Plovers Cottage is just round the corner from the church. A substantial rectory adjoins the graveyard, which is rumoured to contain the last resting place of Elizabethan adventurer Anthony Jenkinson who travelled all the known world, including Russia, only to die in Teigh in 1611 whilst visiting the squire. Bad luck, Tony, but Teigh has to be a better place to expire than Vladivostok. It's warmer, for a start.

And talking of death, it's a fact that murder most foul took place in this most unlikely setting in the 13th century when a group of armed men rode into town, dragged the then Teigh priest from his church and slew him in the street. The gang was allegedly led by a knight of the realm and the cleric, having borrowed money, hadn't paid his debts. As they say in the best Westerns, he had it coming.

Teigh

MURDER IN A THANKFUL VILLAGE

Alan Oliver.

Langham, three miles north of Oakham on the Melton road, is awash with underground water. More than 40 wells and watercourses are thought to lurk beneath its surface. We found one under our living room when we lived at Langham. My wife tried a spot of water divining and was amazed, and somewhat startled, when the dowsing rods she held in her hands began to twitch with some ferocity. We left shortly afterwards.

The village is bisected by a stream which was once a vital source for the famous Ruddles brewery. It all ended for one of Rutland's oldest employers in the 1990s when the family firm was bought by mega-brewers Greene King after a protracted bid to save it. But big business was always likely to prevail and its once-hallowed site is now occupied by housing.

Langham boasts two polo centres and a lovely little bowling green. It features a grid of little lanes running parallel to each other with the commanding church of Sts Peter & Paul set in spacious grounds which include the old cemetery.

It's fitting that 14th century cleric Simon de Langham was one famous 'old boy who made good'. Born around 1310, Simon was Archbishop of Canterbury from 1366-68 and later Chancellor of England. Others with local links included Henry Norris, arraigned for treason in 1536; and Thomas Cromwell, Henry VIII's somewhat sinister 'eyes and ears' until getting his head chopped off in 1540. In the 1920s Edward, Prince of Wales (later the Duke of Windsor) was known to have stayed in his Langham hunting lodge whilst away with the Cottesmore.

The village's many handsome buildings include Langham Hall, which unfortunately suffered a catastrophic roof fire in 2007. There is no village shop but two pleasant, yet differing, pubs – the Wheatsheaf and the Noel Arms – stand cheek by jowl while the old village school building is currently a private house enhanced by railway artefacts.

Not far away is Ranksborough Hall – former home of the Marquis of Londonderry with its grounds today tastefully dotted with housing – and Barleythorpe Hall, former home of the bluff 'yellow earl' Lord Lonsdale, the originator of boxing's Lonsdale Belt, who was described by a fellow peer as 'almost an emperor but not quite a gentleman.' His house and grounds are now the HQ of the Engineering Employers' East Midlands Federation.

Langham

CHURCH STREET

Alan Oliver.

In 1995 Nigel Moon purchased Whissendine windmill and embarked on a major restoration programme. The mill was built of local stone in around 1830 and had four patent sails on a Lincolnshire cross.

During a violent gale in 1922 the sails were broken off and the cross tree broken. Gradual deterioration set in but some repair and maintenance work saved the structure and Nigel, a miller with a history of saving old buildings, bought the mill and began by restoring the ancient stonework and capping its top before bringing the sails into play.

Power is now provided by an electric motor that turns one set of stones and Nigel's grain is much in demand by top bakeries. Mills were once an essential part of village life – another wind-powered mill, also restored by Nigel, stands on a ridge near Wymondham just over the Leicestershire boundary. But at a time when Whissendine was a self-sufficient community, the village relied heavily on the miller's output.

A large mill was once sited in Oakham at the top of the current Mill Street near the town boundary, while the core of a mill  stands on the scarp above Ketton and a fine white mill stands proud on a ridge overlooking Morcott on the Uppingham-Peterborough road, though it has long been converted to private accommodation.

Morcott Windmill

The Whissendine mill is certainly the pick of the revitalised crop, looking down on a settlement that snakes around a loop and crosses a brook. There are two pubs and St Andrew's church is large enough to match the village.

Earliest parts of the church date from the 13th century and the spacious interior features an excellent collection of gargoyles, a medieval wooden screen (brought from the old chapel of St John's College, Cambridge) and a fine Victorian reredos.

One theory is that Rota's Moor between the village and Teigh refers to the man who gave his name to Rutland. Whatever the truth, 18th century locals had to be on their guard in this 'border' country where once footpads roamed at will. One Whissendine parson showed commendable initiative in leaping a gate on his horse after two ruffians had tied it in anticipation of a mugging. Others weren't so fortunate.

Whissendine

TILTING AT WINDMILLS

Alan Oliver

It's an amazing fact that mazes were first thought to have been forms of penance. Rutland had a maze of sorts near Lyddington and another was traced to Medbourne, near Market Harborough – but tiny Wing maze is the great survivor.

Set back from the Glaston road on the outskirts of the village, it features a whorled pathway between a network of raised turves. But although maze walkers will find little mystery in finding their way out of this particular mini-labyrinth – because it's so small - its origins are hazy.

Penance was apparently the done thing in medieval times. The Wing maze was believed to have been devised as part of a pagan ritual but by the Middle Ages it was being used by a cult which exacted heavy penance for perceived sins. Oo-er.

That same swirled pattern appears on Greek coins minted before the birth of Christ. It's also featured on a stained glass window at Rheims in France, and it's thought Wing penitents were just following the trend of the times by shuffling along the maze on their knees whilst chanting incantations. It may have increased one's powers of meditation but it did nowt for arthritis.

And then there's Wing village itself, standing south of Rutland Water and boasting one of the largest water treatment plants in Britain to cleanse the output from the mighty reservoir.

Wing's inhabitants were once known rather unfairly as 'cuckoos' – suggesting alleged stupidity. A traditional jingle suggested 'The folk of Wing tried to hedge the cuckoo in' but I'd heard something similar about Gotham, Notts and that wasn't true either.

One very wise 19th century Wing woman certainly shattered all loony allusions with her capacity for healing the sick. Amelia Woodcock claimed her powers derived from being the seventh daughter of a seventh daughter and encouraged streams of devotees to trek to her cottage to buy her ointments and potions. Alas, when she died in 1867 she was tainted by accusations of witchcraft. Not a great recipe for success. She should have sued.

Wing

A LITTLE AMAZING

Alan Oliver. 08

Hard to imagine they fought over this field. We're 200 yards from the busy A1 motorway, formerly the Great North Road, formerly Ermine Street. It's a bracing spring day and, in the distance, the juggernauts grind by. But here we're among wide, undulating meadows that look largely untouched by history.

Today Loosecoat Field is a peaceful place but 'twas not always so. Five hundred years ago a Wars of the Roses battle was fought here which was gory even by that campaign's bloody standards.

At least 10,000 men died fighting in – or retreating from – a merciless melange of swinging axes, cannon balls and charging horses. The Battle of Loosecoat Field – called the Battle of Horn Field by contemporaries and also known as the Battle of Empingham – involved the Houses of York and Lancaster and took place on March 12th, 1470 at a time when there was much jostling in the shires for King Edward IV's throne.

When Edward heard that Lancastrian Sir Robert Welles (the 8th Baron Willoughby de Eresby) was raising Lincolnshire levies in support of the 'Kingmaker' Earl of Warwick and the claimant Duke of Clarence, he marched from London to meet the rebels who numbered at least 30,000 and were heading south for Stamford.

The mighty forces clashed north of Tickencote Warren near the Rutland-Lincolnshire border, Edward first treating both armies to the execution of Welles' father, the captive – and therefore unfortunate – Lord Welles, and the battle was short and its aftermath grisly.

The Lancastrians were soon running for their lives with the Yorkists cutting down stragglers. The extent of the carnage accounts for one nearby plantation being named Bloody Oaks and local Lancastrian supporters under Pickworth squire Sir John Hussey discarding the distinctive coats bearing Sir John's livery before making a last stand at Pickworth.

Hence Loosecoat Field, though others suggest the name was derived from the Old English 'hlosecot' meaning pigsty cottage. Pickworth was sacked – just one arch of its church remains – and 40 years ago a mass grave was discovered.

Locals reported seeing the ghosts of slain soldiers for many years after the slaughter, but fresh breezes now blow through Loosecoat. I ask a pleasant young receptionist at a nearby office unit if she knew about the site. 'A battle? In that field? 10,000 killed?' she replies, wide-eyed. 'Cool!' Not so much cool as chilling.

Loosecoat

REMAINS OF THE CHURCH

Alan Oliver.

A crisp February day and a pair of stout shoes are essential requirements for a yomp along the switchback road to Preston. Not t'Lancashire mill town, tha knows, though even that must have started out as a single snaking street without a care in t'world.

No, this 'priest's town' is a far quieter prospect – a ridged cluster of tranquillity, amazingly just yards from the busy Oakham-Uppingham highway.

The ideal Sunday stroll, however, starts three miles south in Ayston, tucked away, almost as an afterthought, near Uppingham. Once a royal hunting retreat, the former 'Athelstan's village' still manages to be truly detached, if not aloof.

This sunny Sabbath is unfortunately notable for an excess of car traffic through peaceful lanes. Yet Ayston's score of handsome ironstone buildings – one with a pig weathervane – are bathed in sunlight, snowdrops flourish and all is well at Ayston Hall, where a man and a woman, who may or may not be the owners, play a knockabout game of golf on the sweeping lawns and birds twitter from tall trees.

A rolling lane leads to Ridlington bypassing open fields surrounded by hazy hills. There is much history here – its church is essentially 13th century and the village was once part of

Ayston

the dower of Mercian queens – but few Rutland villages contain so many diverse styles of housing in one short stretch.

And so back to Preston, a gem on the hill which once had two pubs but at the time of writing has none. Shucks! At least the stonework of its many fine houses shine like burnished gold and its church of Sts Peter & Paul boasts exquisite architecture. This 'priest's town' is far closer to the beating heart of England. Do those wicked property developers know it's there?

Preston

FROM AYSTON TO PRESTON

Heaven means different things to different people. If you visit Barrowden on a good day, it's sitting outside the excellent Exeter Arms, sipping its micro-brewery ales and looking out over grassy slopes down to the pretty pond where ducks have their own rafted, roofed home. The village of Wakerley, once a railway halt pre-Beeching, is in the distance.

Barrowden means 'burial ground on the hill' and there's been a settlement here for centuries. It was once a royal manor and boasted a weekly market and an annual fair.

With the Uppingham-Peterborough road passing a mile away further up the hill, 21st century Barrowden has garnered its fair share of big city commuters. But – despite the occasional incursions of 'travelling folk' – it's still far enough off-track to retain its tranquillity. Warm weekends, on the other hand, attract everyone from day-trippers to jazz bands.

Founder of modern tourism Thomas Cook visited Barrowden in the 1830s as part of his role as an itinerant Baptist minister and cabinet-maker and married Marianne Mason of West Farm.

Local characters abound. One 17th century clan – the inappropriately named Goodlad family – were regularly in trouble for not attending church. They also ploughed on saints' days and withheld ecclesiastical dues. The cads.

More recent notables were Eddie Wade, a saddler by trade, and his effervescent wife Winnie who ran Barrowden store in the 1930s and 1940s. Winnie, who also sold toys from a back room, once got into terrible trouble with the village baker for buying her bread, ready wrapped, from Peterborough. These days they'd all be fighting to save the post office as the axe falls, one by one, on rural communities.

One 19th century blacksmith was sufficiently laid-back to laugh at the discovery of a plough tied to his chimney stack, while the clerk to St Peter's church was traditionally paid in eggs until 1900.

The ancient June ceremony of beating the bounds (walking the parish boundaries) was even more curious, with village urchins scrambling for coins deposited in holes in the ground. This was known as 'treacling' because they would later undergo a mock thrashing followed by spoonfuls of treacle all round. All very strange, but then there was no telly in those days.

Barrowden

SHEER BLISS AT BARROWDEN

Whitwell: Twinned With Paris. So says the road sign – and indeed it is, though the French may not be aware of it.

What began as a Sixties pub joke certainly put the village on the map, though Parisians were 'n'amusent pas' at the time and there have been no official twinning visits since.

Yet it still raises a bit of a laugh at the Noel Arms, which used to be a tiny pub frequented by anglers. They, the locals and 'Mr Rutland' himself, the late journalist Eddie Hudson, probably all had a hand in devising the French connection.

The old Noel was a little gem where the ancient landlady would descend to the cellar, at great personal risk, to pull foaming pints from the barrel. But all that, of course, has changed.

One Victorian photo of Whitwell shows a bewhiskered postman standing calmly with a group of lads in the middle of the main road. These days they'd be bowled over as swiftly as a tax rise on 4x4s as the traffic bobs and weaves like dodgem cars through the chicane on the Oakham-Stamford road where the speed limit is allegedly 30mph.

At least St Michael's church still stands secure on its grassy knoll, with its 13th century bellcote, 800-year-old font and a memorial to Charles Ellicott, surely Rutland's longest-serving vicar.

West of Whitwell is Barnsdale, where acclaimed gardening guru Geoff Hamilton based his TV programmes. One journalist of my acquaintance – not Eddie, it was his sidekick Mel – swore that the outlaw Robin Hood operated from round here but somehow I doubt it.

Empingham lies east of Whitwell on the route around Rutland Water. Its White Horse hotel remains a welcoming watering hole for tired ramblers, a worthy successor to medieval Empingham's famous three-day fairs on the feast of St Botolph.

The church of St Peter's is one of the largest in the county as befits an area whose humungous wealth was based on wool. Rumour hath it that some of the houses that line the Tickencote road were built side-on to the highway so their inhabitants couldn't see the passing gentry, but I'm not sure that's any more kosher than seeing Friar Tuck riding a bike with a string of onions round his neck.

Whitwell

TWINNED WITH PARIS

Hambleton and its surrounding settlements once belonged to the Queen of Mercia. Domesday records 750 villagers, three churches and 45 ploughs.

The rise and rise of Rutland Water engulfed the lower Hambletons but Upper Hambleton remained proud on its hill with the splendid Jacobean Old Hall at the water's edge and the church of St Andrew's just across the way from the Finches Arms where wayward wartime servicemen once pinched a copper's bike in the blackout.

Hambleton presents such a picture of perfect peace on a fine day – with walks to the water's edge where the road once ran to Normanton – that it's hard to believe two separate murder incidents happened near here, one the killing of a travelling carter by two brothers in the 19th century – for which felony they were suitably strung up – and the other the Severs case which involved the slaying of a respected father and mother by their son, since imprisoned, in their bungalow home.

Hambleton can be approached either via the rising peninsula road from Oakham or from Egleton. There's something cosy about a village almost surrounded by water. First stop is the aforementioned Finches Arms which overlooks the reservoir in all its glory. Second stop is Hambleton Hall, built 1881, which has TV celebrity Aaron (pronounced Arren) Patterson as its head chef.

The handsome hall is set in its own grounds and was a haunt of high society in the Twenties and Thirties when it was owned by the Astley-Coopers. The playwright, composer and actor Noel Coward first stayed there as a teenager whilst recovering from TB, though it's said his poverty-stricken mother had to pawn her diamond ring to pay young Noel's train fare from London to Oakham.

But that was in 1915 and there were plenty of riches to come from films, plays and a string of West End shows. Coward returned regularly to Hambleton Hall to play piano and entertain – he is believed to have written part of *Blithe Spirit* there – and his jolly songs at the piano were particularly popular with wellwishers who crowded the village hall to hear 'The Master' in full swing. Mad Dogs and Englishmen …

Hambleton

OLD HALL, HAMBLETON

Alan Oliver

The Great North Road has brought many folk to Rutland over the centuries. The Romans founded Great Casterton, though others had been here before. A major military camp was based nearby and the church of Sts Peter and Paul is thought to be on the site of a Roman temple.

1,800 years later and 'Sweet Patty of the Vale' from Casterton became the wife of peasant poet John Clare. The village has long had a reputation for its hospitality and many a weary coaching party bound for Stamford was offered good meals and lodgings before tackling the steep Toll Bar climb.

There's been plenty of news from Casterton over the years. In 1957 a widowed Casterton father and his daughter made national headlines by getting married – not to each other, but in separate ceremonies on the same day. The village was also noted for the quality of its concert parties and entertainments and there are close ties with the Casterton Community College, set high on the road to Ryhall, which has an excellent academic record, particularly in computer studies.

There is, of course, a smaller version of this sprawling settlement called Little Casterton which lies on a delightful lane off the Stamford road. It really is little, with just a scattering of handsome houses hugging the lane that leads to Tolethorpe where the Rutland Open-Air Theatre has its home at the hall.

The remarkable Tolethorpe venture was inspired by the Stamford Shakespeare Company which formerly staged plays in the garden behind the George in Stamford. A labour of love transformed neglected Tolethorpe Hall, originally the 16th century home of the Browne family, into a world famous venue.

The company performs during the summer months and the auditorium is covered to keep out the elements whilst the actors perform in the open-air. It seems to work, with beautiful glades adding to the lustre, but nobody can control the weather. It is, however, the management's proud boast that no performance has ever been cancelled because of the elements – though one performance of *Macbeth* was enlivened by a real thunderstorm and a fox once wandered on stage during *A Midsummer Night's Dream*.

Great Casterton

TOLETHORPE HALL, LITTLE CASTERTON

Most folks' first sight of Ketton is its towering chimneys. Castle Cement's works dominate the landscape, though its stacks could soon be rivalled as landmarks by wind turbines if planning applications go through.

Castle's quarries contain bat caves and prehistoric finds, plus the paw prints of the legendary Rutland Panther – a large and mysterious feline whose existence has yet to be confirmed.

The Romans were probably the first to mine at Ketton, which stands proudly astride a major route for travellers near the confluence of the Chater and Welland. Many of its buildings were built of local limestone, though some were erected with Barnack stone. Nearby Collyweston supplied the slates.

Durable Ketton stone was used for some of Britain's finest buildings including Cambridge University, parts of Westminster Abbey and the cathedrals of Ely and Peterborough. Present day master mason Andre Vrona, who has also worked on projects in London and Cambridge, gladly follows in the famous traditions of young craftsman William Hibbins – only 21 when he died – whose grave in the churchyard is beautifully embellished with carvings of the stonemason's art.

Ketton's appendages are Aldgate and Geeson but it's the main village itself which continues to fascinate. St Mary the Virgin church – close by one of the narrowest road bridges in the county – was partly restored by the great Victorian architect Sir Gilbert Scott and contains an enhanced peal of bells, the work on which the whole community helped fund.

The village primary school has gone from 'special measures' to Ofsted plaudits in quick succession – thanks to a marvellous head teacher and her team – and the Ketton Club is a regular meeting place.

Every village has its quaint customs. In Ketton a bell was formerly rung at 9am and 5pm to tell the gleaners – women and children who collected the harvest – when to enter and leave the fields.

The ancient game of quoits was so popular that there were several 'beds' and a Mr Knox of Ketton was champion of England three years running. And a hiring fair used to be held in November, with those successful allowed a small advance called 'hence money'. Much of it was promptly spent on booze and entertainment, leading to thick ears all round when the lads got home.

Ketton

CHURCH STREET

Alan Oliver. 08

In 2007 a moving ceremony was held in Ashwell church to commemorate a remarkable clergyman.

The Rev James Adams only lived in the village for two years at the very end of his career but his recently enhanced grave in St Mary's churchyard has become a place of pilgrimage. For the 'have-a-go' rector was the first-ever chaplain to be awarded the Victoria Cross, and there are echoes of a current conflict in how he won it.

Born in Ireland, Adams was a padre with the Royal Lancers in Afghanistan in 1866. An excellent horseman, he was accompanying a troop of cavalry when they came under fire as they approached a muddy ditch. At least three soldiers had their horses killed beneath them but Adams had no hesitation in dragging the animals' bodies to one side while he rescued the men and led them to safety through a hail of bullets. It was a superhuman effort and Army commander 'Bobs' Roberts instantly recommended him for the VC.

Adams later took over a Suffolk parish before moving to Ashwell where he lived at the rectory until his death in 1903. A memorial book listing Adams' exploits is currently on display inside the church.

Another famous Ashwellian was Beryl Markham, the first woman pilot to fly east-west solo across the Atlantic in 1936. But an even more remarkable character was 17th century rector and ardent Royalist Thomas Mason who was expelled from the parish for his beliefs during the English Civil War but went on to command a company in the King's army and act as escort to Charles I. He was reinstated as rector in 1660 after an absence of 16 years.

Ashwell was originally part of the estates of that same King Harold who was slain at Hastings. Much of it lies compactly between St Mary's church, the Oakham road and a brook and it includes many fine houses. An ancient spring still refreshes travellers but, sadly, there is no pub to cater for stronger tastes.

Ashwell

THE VICAR VC

Alan Oliver

The stump of a market cross in the Edith Weston square is a reminder that Edward the Confessor gave the village to his Queen Edith as a royal dower, hence the name.

The square, tucked away in the heart of the village, is where it all started in the 11th century. St Mary's church (just round the corner) dates from Norman times and, like many a country church, was greatly expanded. It's a pity no-one anticipated a 20th century decline in worshippers.

The former air base at North Luffenham – now St George's Barracks and the home of a Royal Artillery regiment – was once a cushy billet for singer Matt Monroe in his service days. The village of North Luffenham is about a mile or so away. Archdeacon Robert Johnson, founder of both Oakham and Uppingham schools, lived here in the 16th century and is commemorated with a brass wall plaque in St John's church. His son Abraham was high sheriff in 1618 and rector for 21 years and the churchyard contains some 40 Commonwealth war graves. Luffenham Hall is a handsome building with impressive gates.

Not far away is South Luffenham, where a young Hermann Goering once attended private school. The blighter loved the area, even having the gall to play golf at Luffenham Heath in the early 1930s.

Three miles west along the ridge from Edith Weston lies Manton, a stopping-off point for numerous walkers, cyclists and runners tackling the round-Rutland Water trackway.

Manton sits astride a railway tunnel – though you'd never have thought it – and for many years was an important railway halt, from which trains could be caught to, or emptied from, London St Pancras. Many a chinless fop arrived from 'the Smoke' for hunting weekends when Prime Minister Herbert Henry Asquith was in residence at the Grange.

Times have changed but Manton remains its dreamily quaint self. Two elderly sisters who bought adjoining houses were known to have knocked a hole between the two structures so they could see more of each other.

Edith Weston

NAMED FOR A QUEEN

A significant number of grand houses and elegant mansions continue to grace Rutland, though many are no longer family homes.

Belton-in-Rutland in the south-west of the county has a fine Old Hall which, together with ancient farmhouses, suggests it was a prosperous farming community when agriculture had a future. The unfortunate Charles I is reputed to have rested here following his defeat at Naseby.

Seaton also has a substantial building – its Manor House – while village visitors can take in views of the marvellous Victorian rail viaduct across the valley to Harringworth.

Glaston, a few miles north on the A47, includes several remarkable old houses down Manor Lane, some with mullioned windows, in addition to a hall now divided into offices for hi-tech companies.

Gunthorpe's hall was, until recently, occupied by Col Tom Haywood, a former lord-lieutenant of Rutland who wore military uniform for Remembrance Day ceremonies right into his 80s. Ghosts – not including Col Haywood – are said to lurk on the main road below. Crayfish certainly thrive in nearby streams en route to Brooke.

Thorpe-by-Water's manor house is known as Tudor House and some say a church was once located a little to the east.

Morcott's Priest's House dates from 1627 and Tinwell has a Manor House which was allegedly once the dower house of the Cecils of Burghley. The 'hidden gem' of Tixover also boasts handsome buildings set on a pre-Roman site with a blacksmith's forge with a horseshoe-shaped entrance. The village centrepiece is St Mary Magdalen church which boasts an impressive tower arch.

Sadly some magnificent houses are no longer with us. Top of the list is Springfield which once stood on the Ashwell road. Once the home of Lord and Lady Londonderry, it had strong Royal connections and, during the First World War, staged a national land girls' harvesting competition. Its water gardens were much admired but it was allowed to fall into disrepair before demolition.

Cottesmore Hall was also a fine building in its time, being adjacent to the hunt kennels. The Marchioness of Bute delighted local children by distributing sweets, holding parties and riding her Egyptian donkey Pharoah round the grounds. The Hall caught fire not once but twice and was eventually razed to make way for housing.

Halls and Mansions

GLASTON HALL

Alan Oliver.

Rutland – History and People

Rutland began life as Roteland, some say. In which case its heart could be pinned near Whissendine where an area called Roteland existed for many years. Roteland has been interpreted as 'red land' – a description of the reddish clay soil, as in other place names like Radcliffe and Radley – but whatever its origin, the area was mentioned as such in the Domesday survey of 1086, though not as a county. That was to be 200 years later.

The original Rutland was a sort of buffer zone between Nottinghamshire, Leicestershire, Northamptonshire and Lincolnshire. Nothing much different there then – heavenly Rutters is still Elysium compared with the twin Babels of Nottingham and Leicester.

To the north were the districts of Alstoe and Martinsley, which belonged to the Sheriff of Nottingham (wicked or otherwise), and to the south was Witchley which stretched as far as the gen-

tle Welland. The first recorded maps – centuries later – show the county, as it later became, divided into the administrative Hundreds of Alstoe, Okehamsoke, Martinsley, Wrandyke and Eastern Hundred.

As Bryan Waites points out in his excellent little book *Exploring Rutland,* the area in medieval times was thick with forest and made excellent hunting country. Landowners included the King and the Countess of Huntingdon and those who fell foul of the law were dealt with severely.

In 1269 Peter de Neville, the Lord of Leighfield Manor – which stood within the forest – was declared an outlaw after being found guilty of several offences. They included taking brushwood, timber and acorns; keeping dogs to poach forest game; imprisoning poachers and taking fines which should have gone to the King; illegally charging a toll for safe passage and allowing 300 pigs to pasture illegally. Did he join Robin Hood

– who, some fancifully claim, had a hideout near Barnsdale? Or did he open an acorn supermarket? We shall never know.

Oakham, Hambleton and Ridlington were deemed royal manors. Some of the settlements mentioned in *Domesday* were in sheltered glades among woodland and a handful of them have long since disappeared, including Horn, Alestanestorp, Scultorp and Snelston. Was it the plague, crop failure or just plain ennui that sent them packing? One century they were there – villains, ploughs and all. The next they'd gone. Curious.

The total population of the area in 1086 was around 7,000 – little more than half of Oakham today – and substantial tracts of meadowland were recorded in all villages except Horn, Ryhall and Thistleton. Of the 19 mills mentioned in *Domesday,* Empingham had 12. Present day villages such as Barrow, Clipsham and Pickworth, didn't get a mention. All we know is that Rutland was deficient in fishponds and lacked both markets and borough status.

Halfway along the Braunston-Knossington road – near Rutland's highest point which is around 650ft – was the centre of the Royal Forest of Leighfield close to the medieval deer park of Flitteris and south of another deer park at Cold Overton.

Royal visits were frequent. Henry I reportedly hunted hinds in 'Leigh Forest' where a Sergeant Hasculf was mentioned as keeper of the Forest of Rutland – a big job for one man, one might have thought. Richard I and King William of Scotland met in Rutland in 1194 to discuss the boundary dispute between their two countries and King John was said to have stayed in Preston on one of his grand tours that eventually led him to lose his treasure in the Wash and die from a surfeit of lamfreys. Another notable visitor was Henry VIII who, with his latest Queen, Katherine Howard, spent some days at the Bishop's Palace at Lyddington in 1542 en route from London to Lincoln.

The Gwash stream – which was to play such a vital part 500 years later in sourcing Rutland Water – was Roteland's main waterway, flowing from the liassic uplands of east Leicestershire to meet the Welland near Stamford. It's hardly surprising that settlements grew up along its banks. Remains of an Iron Age fort were found near its headwaters and excavations preceding the creation of Rutland Water uncovered two Roman settlements, an Anglo Saxon farm, a cemetery from the same period containing 160 skeletons – many of them teenagers – and a medieval village.

Rutland arrived as a county in the 13th century and has since stoutly maintained its separate identity.

The smallest county in England was allocated two Members of Parliament until the Redistribution of Seats Act of 1885 brought it down to one. The first mention of any MPs comes in the 'First Complete English Parliament' of 1295 which consisted of elected knights, citizens and burgesses and met in London in November of that year. Robert of Flinkesthorp and Simon of Buckminster appear to have been Rutland's representatives.

The county's more famous names – like the wealthy wool merchant and philanthropist Roger Flore, who was appointed Speaker of the House in 1416, and Everard Digby of Stoke Dry – emerge as MPs during the 15th century and by the 16th century we are on even more familiar ground with local landowners like the Haringtons, Sapcotes, Noels and Finches regularly representing Rutland.

In the 17th century Parliament was regarded as a hindrance by Charles I who called it and suspended it at will, using it largely to rubber-stamp expenses for one cavalier expedition after another. Cromwell, of course, took a different angle entirely and one Rutland MP, Abel Barker, felt the Roundhead's wrath by being excluded from Parliament in 1656.

The first 'Parliament of the Glorious Restoration of King Charles II' in 1660 was attended by Philip Sherard of Whissendine, the second son of Lord Sherard. He was joined by Samuel Browne who had previously been unseated as MP for Bedfordshire.

MPs during the 19th century included the Hon. Charles George Noel, Sir Gilbert Heathcote and the Rt. Hon. G. H. Finch. Those representing Rutland and Stamford during the 20th century included Lord Willoughby de Eresby and Messrs Robert Conant and Kenneth Lewis and – with the constituency now renamed Melton and Rutland – Michael Latham and Alan Duncan, of whom more later.

The first Lord Lieutenant was Francis Hastings, 2nd Earl of Huntingdon, in 1550. The first Sheriff dates from 1129. The title of Lord of the Manor has reposed with the Hanbury family for some years. Current recipient is Joss Hanbury of Burley-on-the-Hill who has welcomed the Queen and Prince Charles to Rutland in recent years and accepted their donations of horseshoes to add to the other cherished specimens of equine footwear to be hung in Oakham Castle.

Until 1974 the county was split into three districts. They were represented by Oakham Rural District Council, which was housed in the grounds of Catmose where the current county council has its home, Uppingham Rural District Council which met at a building in Orange Street and Ketton Rural District Council which met at St Mary's Hill, Stamford.

The first indications that Rutland might lose its coveted status as an independent county had come in 1947 when the Government of the day proposed to redefine county boundaries throughout England and Wales and suggested Rutland should be absorbed into a larger neighbouring authority.

"A bigger unit won't make for efficiency," warned Lord Gainsborough of Exton while Alderman Royce Turner, a local auctioneer, called it "a glaring example of a scheme drawn up from the map and from the map alone." A vociferous public meeting was held at Oakham cinema at which a local farmer called for 'The Boundary Men' to do some useful work instead down the mines or on 'one of our fine farms'. Not surprisingly, the Government wisely decided not to proceed further.

However the issue bounced back in 1959 when the chairman of the Local Government Commission visited Rutland and met with council dignitaries led by Sir Kenneth Ruddle and town clerk Alan Bond. The commission's report was eagerly awaited and when it was published in March 1960 all hell broke loose. It recommended the 'splitting of Rutland to adjoining counties' and started a three-year battle, led by the then MP Kenneth Lewis (later Sir Kenneth) to preserve the status quo which was

not resolved until Tory Home Secretary Sir Keith stood up in Parliament in August 1963 and proclaimed that Rutland was unique and would be left alone.

Mr Lewis earned much praise from grateful Rutlanders, as did Sir Kenneth Ruddle, Lady Thelma Martin, Sir Henry Tate (a scion of the Tate and Lyle sugar company), Sir David Davenport-Handley of Clipsham Hall and Oakham printer and publisher Charles Matkin.

But in 1972 it all started again when the Local Government Reform Act decided Rutland should cease to exist as an administrative county and be absorbed into Leicestershire from April 1974. Independence was restored, as a unitary authority, in 1997 by the John Major government which had to listen to some powerful lobbying and oratory from local councillors led by Eddie Martin and Brian Montgomery.

Eddie – described by one contemporary as being 'both brisk and brusque' – was head of business studies and industrial liaison at Oakham School but it was as leader of Rutland District Council that he made regular delegation trips to the House of Lords to protest the county's case.

"I thought it was an injustice being lumped in with Leicestershire," he told me soon after independence. "Rutland had administratively been wiped off the map." Some folk claimed 'Fast Eddie' had made independence a one-man bandwagon but he always maintained: "You didn't need to meander down every path to make a decision. I acted decisively, not impulsively. We had 20 councillors on the RDC but you can't lead anyone where they don't want to go."

He went on the radio to promote Rutland's case – "First Rutland, then Scotland" he once said famously – and when he returned from the Lords to Rutland on a cold February morning it was to bring news that independence was going through.

April 1, 1997 was the big day and the celebrations started right on cue. They included a huge firework display, a balloon race, street parties and a walk right around Rutland. '*Remember Rutland*' Bryan Waites had written in a tome supporting the county's glories in its hour of need. When the time was right to celebrate, thousands did.

For a county that's a mere speck on the map, little Rutland has spawned some interesting characters over the years.

Starting, maybe, with St Tibba of Ryhall – the 8th century patron saint of hunters and falconers – and moving on to present day like TV celebrities Penny Smith, whose family lived in Lyddington, and Julia Bradbury, who was brought up in Edith Weston – and whose family still lives there - the 'horse-shoe county' has been called home by assorted politicians, artists, musicians and the occasional rogue over the years.

The great and good have stomped its pastures over the centuries – some, like Cromwell's militia, arriving without invitation – and I've been singularly fortunate to have met some of the best in recent years.

Some have been idiosyncratic to the extreme, others dysfunctional, most amazingly normal, but all have shared one thing – a tremendous pride in county. That superb local historian Tony Traylen, who sadly died earlier this year, once published a history of the *Notable Citizens of Rutland,* subtitled A Compendium of the Famous Through to the Infamous.

They're all there – an unrivalled A-Z of Rutlanders past and present – and though I can't hope to compete with Tony's wisdom and meticulous research I can humbly try to bring some of these colourful denizens to life and place them in the context of a shire whose picturesque scenery many of them would recognise today.

If we're starting with Tibba – the original wild child daughter of an Earl of Mercia turned beneficent abbess – then it's only a hop, skip and jump, relatively speaking, to Simon de Langham who was successively Abbot of Westminster, Archbishop of Canterbury from 1366-68 and Chancellor of England.

Clearly a local boy 'dun good', Simon must have wielded enormous influence from afar in troubled times. The fact that he continued to make donations to his tiny village church whilst in high office illustrates not just his humble piety but an enduring affection for his birthplace.

Journalists often ponder how they would interview the 'greats' of the past. Would Beethoven have heard a word I said? Would Richard III have got the hump? Would Elgar have chuntered 'Can't stop now, m'boy, I'm off to the races'? Yet any hack worth his salt would have loved to have met Simon – though perhaps not the aforementioned Tibba, who I suspect might have been a wild-haired Christian of uncertain temperament.

But no. Simon, I suspect, would have been different, spilling the ecclesiastical beans in Heaven's waiting room about his rise from humble farm boy to running the nation's business.

Those were, of course, the days before spin doctors and PR, though I suspect at least one dodgy Oakhamian could have done with both. Titus Oates, not to be confused with the gallant 'Titus' Oates of Scott's 1912 Antarctic expedition, was an unbelievable prig – unbelievable in the sense that nobody in their right mind should have believed a word he said.

The rector's son with *'the face of a haddock and one of the biggest chins in Europe'* exploited late 17th century fears of a Catholic accession to the throne for his own advancement and created mayhem throughout Britain with a 'Papist Plot' that never was.

Titus looms from history like a cross between Arthur Daley and Arthur Mullard, and he certainly fooled a lot of people a lot of the time. Like his father Samuel – who, despite his Christian ministry, was a similar rascal who was chucked in the River Chelmer for ravishing a servant maid – Titus seemed to confuse the sacred and profane to suit his fancy.

To recap, it was 1678 and Oates was sowing his cereals in London having lied his way through his studies at Cambridge, being expelled from a Navy chaplaincy for 'damnably low morals', being axed from the Duke of Norfolk's select band of clergy and enjoying the fleshpots of Castille and Santander. What a rotter.

He had earlier become a Roman Catholic and was befriended by two high-ranking Jesuit priests – Fathers Whitbread and Pickering – whom he would later incriminate and send to the gallows as part of the 'plot.' Nice one, Titus. We might recognise other similarly odious characters to Oates in today's society as there are always unscrupulous people around to take maximum advantage of whipped-up scandal, hubris and hearsay. These days they're called merchant bankers. Or estate agents. Or journalists. Or MPs. Whatever their titles, Oates could have led them a merry dance.

When news spread of a dastardly Jesuit plot to not only assassinate King Charles II – and substitute his Catholic brother the Duke of York on the throne – but to set fire to London and string up as many prominent Protestants as could be found, Oates was hailed as a hero in revealing the 'plot' and alerting the Crown.

In fact he and a team of blackguard associates had instigated the scheme in the first place and 'Chinese whispers' and faked evidence had won him friends in high places who thought he was the saviour of the nation. The witchcraft mentality of the times was conducive to anti-Catholic hysteria. Names were named as being part of the plot and show trials organised – some of them under the notorious 'hanging judge' George Jeffreys.

Three dozen leading Catholics were executed by various means and others jailed. As a chief informer of their 'guilt' and a prosecutor of their innocence, Oates – a gifted and convincing orator – was granted a vast sum of £1,200 a year as a pension before the tide began to turn and the Duke of York brought a civil suit for damages against the Oakham man, alleging defamatory language.

Titus was found guilty, was told to pay £100,000 and, when he couldn't, was thrown into a debtors' prison. The full payback came later when he was found guilty of perjury, whipped and imprisoned for life only to be reprieved on the accession of William and Mary.

He later regained some of his losses by marrying a wealthy widow but he never returned to Rutland, preferring to retire to Westminster where he died in 1705. If ever a film deserved to be made about one of Britain's most notorious rogues, this is it. I could even suggest a well-known writer and present-day rascal called Jeffrey to do the screenplay.

And talking of Jeffreys, we move seamlessly on to Jeffrey Hudson – someone Oakhamians really could be proud of – whose story could also make an excellent movie, though the film's producers might have problems with the lead casting, assuming Danny de Vito was unavailable.

Known as the 'Dwarf of Rutland' because he was barely 3ft 6in tall, Jeffrey was actually a proportionate midget who was born in 1612 to normal-sized parents. He would have been described in today's politically correct jargon as 'vertically challenged' – if he hadn't run you through with his sword beforehand.

What a character! You didn't get much meat to the pound with Big Jeff but you certainly got bags of entertainment. A quick-tempered but charming little chap, he lived his life to the full before dying at a ripe old age. He, like Titus Oates, was a Roman Catholic but there the similarity ends though both were to meet briefly during the feverish days following the alleged Papish Plot.

Jeffrey's father was a humble butcher who fast ingratiated himself with Royal favourite the Duke of Buckingham who lived at Burley-on-the-Hill. Mr Hudson was required by the Duke to breed and keep bulls for the barbaric sport of bull baiting, and it was only a matter of time before the teenage Jeffrey was introduced to the duchess who no doubt thought him quite sweet, took him into service, clothed him in satin and eventually appointed two servants to attend him.

He became an expert swordsman and horseman. He was also groomed as an ardent Royalist, his first party trick being to hide inside a large cold meat pie and spring out to surprise King Charles I and Queen Henrietta Maria at a famous banquet at Burley, whereupon he became a page at court.

One of his tasks was to convey messages for the Queen and a voyage to France on her behalf led to his ship being ambushed by Flemish freebooters and the lad himself being incarcerated at Dunkirk before being brought back to Britain. He later showed his military prowess in a cameo role with the Prince of Orange's army at the siege of Breda in Holland. If the stories are to be believed, the enemy thought a riderless horse was galloping towards them until Jeffrey emerged from behind its mane, sword in hand.

When the English Civil War broke out in 1642 Hudson was made a captain in the King's Horse and gallantly escorted the Queen and her entourage to the Continent for her personal safety and to raise money for the Royalist cause. On their return two years later he helped the Queen elude a Parliamentary cordon at Exeter and return to France.

His career being upwardly mobile – sorry, Jeff, an unfortunate choice of words - he mixed with the finest at the French court. Many of them were ousted Cavaliers who had several grudges to bear after defeat in the Civil War and when one of the oafs picked on Jeffrey and challenged him to a duel the latter shot him dead – the lesson being to always to pick on someone your own size.

Hudson was threatened with imprisonment for the killing but he was protected by the Queen and forced to flee France. Unfortunately he was yet again captured by pirates and this time sold into slavery. He managed to get back to London by 1658 where he lived quietly in the country after the Restoration, returning to Rutland briefly but finally settling in London where, as a Catholic, he was held on suspicion of complicity in the Papish Plot as engineered by his fellow Oakhamian Titus Oates. A small world, indeed.

Swiftly released when Oates' deception was uncovered, Jeffrey was granted a royal pension for life and died in 1682. Numerous portraits were painted of him throughout his lifetime and a stone effigy thought to be of Hudson in armour is kept at the Boathouse Bar at Portumna, Galway of all places.

More than a century before, Robert Johnson had been born in Stamford. It was 1541 and Robert's father Maurice was a prosperous master dyer as well as having served as the town's MP.

Maurice died when his son was ten and the lad went to live with relatives at Peterborough, studying at King's School before taking a BA at Cambridge University where he became a Fellow of Trinity College. So far, so good – and it got better when he followed three years of study in Paris by becoming Chaplain Examiner to the Lord Keeper of the Seal and helping to found Jesus College, Cambridge.

The two mainstays in Johnson's life were education and religion, and the immense patronage of two of the most powerful people in the land – Queen Elizabeth I and her Chancellor Lord Burghley – helped him climb the rungs to success.

In 1574 he arrived in Rutland to become rector of North Luffenham – a post he was to hold until his death in 1625 – and subsequently became Archdeacon of Leicester. But it was his immense foresight in establishing two prestigious schools in Rutland which ensured Robert Johnson's unique place in local history has been preserved unblemished for five centuries.

The twin seats of learning were at Oakham and Uppingham. They were founded in 1584 in modest brownstone Tudor buildings, which still stand today, and both grew to become two of the finest public schools in Britain. Present day scholars at both schools annually hold Founder's Days in grateful remembrance of a man who was a visionary of his time.

Puritanical by faith and modest in lifestyle, Johnson became an outstanding Rutland benefactor by not only founding the two 'free' schools but by re-founding the previously deteriorating Chapel of St John and St Anne in Oakham and creating Hospitals of Christ for elderly townsfolk to live out their twilight years.

Such singular philanthropy was remarkable in an age of grinding poverty and can only hint at Johnson's personal wealth and his enthusiastic persuasion in gaining the support not only of his patrons and local landowners but also of influential figures in the community.

Not since wool merchant Roger Flore's immense contributions to Oakham life – particularly to the church of All Saints and the St John/St Anne's hospital – had Rutland seen such an injection of hands-on munificence. Flore, who died in 1480, had been Speaker of four 15th century Parliaments and also had friends in high places. But even he paled into the shade compared with Johnson who was an extraordinary pioneer in early education. His statue occupies a niche in the main façade of Uppingham School, proudly holding – as befits the man – a miniature version of the original Elizabethan building which stands in solitary splendour the other side of St Peter and St Paul church a short distance away.

The annals of Uppingham School include many fine headmasters who enhanced each stage of academic development

with their presence. Edward Thring sounds like a Goon Show character who might have been voiced by Harry Secombe in his prime, but there was nothing goonish about the man who was head at Uppingham from 1853 to 1887 and for many years was mentioned in the same breath as Dr Thomas Arnold, Rugby School's educational evangelist, later to be immortalised by Thomas Hughes in the novel *Tom Brown's Schooldays*.

Thring really was a vigorous reformer of the highest order. He was born in Alford, Somerset in 1821 and died in 1887 and his motto was 'Honour the work and the work will honour you.' He believed that healthy minds should be complemented by healthy bodies and, at his insistence; Uppingham was the first public school in Britain to establish a gymnasium.

Thring was also the first head teacher to organise a regional conference of his peers to debate the latest developments in education. Not surprisingly the first session was held at his home and 37 academics attended. The dramatic increase in pupil intake numbers at Uppingham during Thring's tenure reflect both his overwhelming influence and his administrative enthusiasm in attracting the best teachers and getting more and more youngsters into education. When he first arrived the school had just 25 boys on its roll. Within 20 years the figure had grown to 300, by which time his subtle innovations and powerful personality had ensured it national acclaim.

One incident in 1875 sums up the stature of the man. Concerned about the outbreak of a feverish illness in Uppingham and its effects upon his flock, Thring resolved to move pupils, staff and household lock, stock and barrel to the seaside to escape the epidemic. It was an evacuation of almost Biblical proportions and the resourceful Thring acted with incredible speed to organise the extraordinary rescue mission which transported all of them to Borth on the Cardiganshire coast where, within days, they were settling in and relishing the sea air.

Thring had commandeered a disused hotel and assorted seaside boarding houses and, although his scholars must have welcomed the chance to indulge in bracing walks and build sandcastles during term time, the head vowed that lessons should continue unabated. No saucy seaside postcards, lads, if you please.

When the fresh-faced pupils and their 30 teachers reported back at Uppingham after the epidemic had passed, Thring was able to confirm that educational standards had indeed been maintained. The episode became part of school folk lore and the fortuitous move to Borth is commemorated to this day by an annual service in the school chapel.

Hugh 5th Earl of Lonsdale was, at first glance, the sort of quality geezer who used to be played by Roger Livesey in British film comedies.

Schoolchildren gathered around his shooting brake to present him and his wife with flowers – invariably a gardenia for his buttonhole – and his liveried staff were almost perennially garbed in yellow, giving the old boy the epithet The Yellow Earl. But although he played the benign landowner to the hilt, the larger than life 'Lordy' Lonsdale was also a bit of a pug. In his youth he boxed and once gave the great heavyweight champion John L. Sullivan a sound thrashing in a catchweight bout. The Lonsdale Belt, which is still strapped round the sweated waists of British boxing champions at the end of bouts, was his idea and bears his likeness along with other punch-drunk dignitaries who liked to 'tip the claret.'

Rutland has been home to many noble families – and still is – but the late Victorian/early Edwardian period was the zenith of the 'house party' aristocracy ahead of the shattering rearrangement of society that came in the wake of the First World War.

The Lonsdales had made their money from coal and although Hugh's ancestral home was at Lowther Castle he spent so much time at his Rutland pad, Barleythorpe Hall, that he became an essential member of the local huntin', shootin' boxin' set.

In some ways, Barleythorpe was impressed upon him. A free-spender all his life, this megabucks magnifico was persuaded by the trustees of his estate to curb some of his excesses by concentrating his activities on his 'more modest' country home which stood – and still stands – in some splendour off the Oakham-Langham road.

Few peers were as adventurous as 'Lordy' who roughed it in the Klondyke gold rush, fought in the Boer war, invested – disastrously – in a cattle farm in Wyoming and became great friends with the Kaiser with whom he shared a birth date and a liking for yellow limousines. The Automobile Association adopted the colour when he became its first president.

When not wearing hunting pink or shooting jackets, 'Lordy' favoured a frock coat, spats and shiny topper in which to be driven to formal occasions. He was a familiar figure at Ascot races – when he would arrive in a yellow landau complete with postillions wearing yellow jackets, golden top hats, white buckskin breeches and black leather boots. He became a confidante of the equally bluff King Edward VII, who also smoked huge cigars and liked the fillies.

Born in 1857, Hugh's life was devoted to breeding and racing horses. He succeeded to the earldom on the death of his brother George and married Grace, daughter of the Marquess of Huntly. The couple were disconsolate when she lost their only child during pregnancy following a hunting accident but they threw themselves with increasing vigour into the social whirl, entertaining Royalty and nobility at Barleythorpe, Lowther and their other homes in London. When the First World War was declared, Hugh raised a detachment of 1,000 men whom he called the Lonsdales to fight on the Western Front.

Ever the showman, he was a great man for arranging 'spectaculars' such as a re-creation of his Lowther Castle gardens at the 1910 Royal Horse Show at Olympia which involved 50,000 potted plants. But the money began to run out in the 1920s. An £80,000 a year allowance was frittered away and Barleythorpe Hall was sold, as was Lowther Castle. The once-flamboyant 5th Earl of Lonsdale, who had once insisted on being accompanied on his journeys from house to house by a full 25-piece orchestra, was eventually reduced to living in just one property – Stud House near Oakham.

He died in 1944, a character to the last. His loyal wife, Grace, had died two years before. They were both greatly respected in the Rutland community and are still remembered as – somewhat shaky – pillars of society by those former schoolchildren who met them and by the descendants of those who greatly appreciated them as employers. So the world turns…

Another all-action toff – though not such an infinitely and all-embracing big beast as Hugh Lonsdale – was Beryl Markham, the first woman pilot to fly solo from Britain to the American continent.

As related in Mary Lovell's biography *Straight On Till Morning,* Beryl was born in Ashwell in 1902, the daughter of a Flaming Ferrari of a father who was cashiered from the King's Scottish Borderers following an incident involving either fast women, slow horses or cash flow problems – or possibly all three.

The family didn't stay long in Ashwell – though the feisty Beryl often came back for the hunting – preferring to chance their collective arms instead in British East Africa where father Clive bred and raced horses. His wife, however, was soon back in Britain, preferring to run a genteel teashop in Melton Mowbray where things were a good deal quieter.

In her teens, Beryl became part of the louche Happy Valley set which included *Out of Africa* principals Karen Blixen and Denys Finch-Hatton. She returned to London to be presented at court, aged 26, and to mix with a crowd which included Prince Henry, later Duke of Gloucester, but her heart was in Kenya where her father had won every major horse race and she herself rode with great zest when not killing things on safari.

Having seduced Lord Delamere's son in the family stables, she then made a play for wealthy Mansfield Markham who became the first of her three husbands, thereby relieving her of the unpretentious family surname of Clutterbuck. She took up flying in her late 20s, gaining her pilot's licence in 1932 and immediately sniffing around for a challenge.

A fop at a cocktail party prompted her to make history by reminding her that the American Amelia Earhart had already flown the Atlantic west-east in 15 hours and wouldn't it be nice if Beryl could do the trip in reverse. Always one for a challenge, the angular aviatrix asked one of Britain's top aeronautical designers to create a suitable plane and, one wet and windy day in September 1936 she took off for America armed only with a radio, a bottle of brandy and a handful of nuts.

Having barely cleared a row of trees at the end of the runway, her 200hp De Havilland-powered Vega Gull – dubbed The Messenger - ran straight into headwinds and scattered storms. Her radio packed up and she had to use blind-flying instruments. Then a fuel tank ran dry and she had to fly 300ft above the unwelcoming Atlantic until the supply kicked in.

Bruised, battered but eternally defiant, she eventually crash-landed in Cape Breton, Newfoundland after 22 hours of flying where a farmer who found her remembers her saying snootily:

"I've just flown from England. I'm expected in Nova Scotia. Kindly get someone to send me a taxi."

Once her head cuts were treated, Beryl was transported inland before progressing to the United States itself where, dressed in her traditional slacks, scarf and shirt, she was greeted by rapturous crowds and the pint-sized mayor of New York, Fiorello La Guardia.

Things were never quite as exciting again and her latter years were spent in reasonably active retirement in Kenya where she died, aged 84, fighting the inevitable to the last. Beryl Markham's life was spent at the gallop and although she made many enemies with her forthright manner she also made many friends who stood by her at times of crises – of which there were many.

Winning the Grand National is the dream of every owner, trainer and jockey – and the late Frank Gilman of Morcott achieved this in 1982 with Grittar, ridden by Mr Dick Saunders.

It was a tough old race around Aintree's fearsome obstacles but at least the homely Grittar did considerably better than Another Rake, another of Gilman's charges, who fell in the 1957 race. The White Horse pub at Morcott was heaving with well-wishers for weeks after Grittar's triumph while the equine hero was as pleased as punch to be left to his own devices in the pasture.

Frank was born at Pickworth into a farming family and played rugby for Oakham School. Following a serious illness he was advised to exercise his wasted muscles by riding horses. He joined the Cottesmore Hunt and eventually became chairman of the Cottesmore point-to-point. Apart from breeding stars like Grittar, he also enjoyed a game of cricket and became chairman of Oakham Cricket Club.

The Russian Revolution of 1917 saw many émigrés heading west to escape the Bolshevik terror. Prince Yuri Galitzine was born in Japan in 1918 en route to London where his father was an assistant military attaché. After brief sojourns in Austria and France the family finally settled in England where Yuri took up an apprenticeship with Fairey Aviation.

When the Second World War broke out, he joined the Middlesex Regiment and later the Royal Northumberland Fusiliers, and served in the North Africa campaign. He was with the US 45th Division on D-Day as a member of its propaganda unit and accompanied the armies through France and across the Rhine, later becoming involved with War Crimes Commission. "I saw some terrible things on my journeys," he said later at his Clipsham home. "There were so many atrocities in the aftermath of war."

In peacetime he pursued a business career, becoming regional vice-president of an international group, which comprised 88 companies, and being made a Fellow of the Institute of Public Relations.

When I met him, shortly before his death, he was a leading light in the Rutland Local History and Record Society with an encyclopaedic knowledge of the county reinforced by a huge library in his living room. A dignified man, with a gentle sense of humour, he was formerly chairman of the Rutland Record Society.

Gardening guru Geoff Hamilton brought fame to Rutland in the 1980s with TV programmes from Barnsdale which combined an informative approach with a relaxed and friendly style. Millions of people watched his shows and there was great regret when he died suddenly in 1996 at the height of his career. The popular Barnsdale Garden Centre on Exton Avenue is his legacy.

Others to have made their mark on Rutland over the centuries include William Whiston of Lyndon (d. 1752), a mathematician who predicted that a comet would hit the Earth at 5.05am on Wednesday October 14th, 1712, burning all in its path. His prediction sparked widespread panic, including a run on the banks, but although the comet arrived in the Earth's atmosphere at the right time it passed by harmlessly. Nice try but no cigar.

Thomas Barker, who married Whiston's daughter and also lived at Lyndon, was described as the 'father of meteorology'. In 1796 he recorded ten days of 'abnormally smokey' weather at Lyndon which was later linked to a huge volcanic eruption in Iceland.

George Phillips hit the headlines by being the owner of the first car, an 8hp Decauville, to be registered in Rutland. He also edited the *Rutland Magazine* from 1903 to 1924, started an 8,000-volume lending library and wrote a definitive history of Rutland in the Great War before dying in 1922. His name lives on through the George Phillips architectural award.

Incidentally, a Mr B A Adams of Oakham was not only the proud possessor of the very first registration number in Rutland – FP1, for a motor cycle – but the first registered telephone number, Oakham 2, which was listed in the name of B A Adams and Sons, solicitors, in 1906. There was, apparently, no Oakham 1 available.

Edmond Bonner, one-time rector of Uppingham, was King Henry VIII's envoy to Rome in the delicate matter of that out-size monarch's divorce from Catherine of Aragon. Like many a churchman, he ended up in jail during Elizabeth I's reign, dying at Marshalsea prison, aged 69, in 1569.

Another clergyman, Dr Alexander Gill, who later became an usher at Oakham School, very nearly suffered the same fate. Having fallen out with the Archbishop of Canterbury in the 1620s, he was bizarrely sentenced to losing both his ears – one to be segmented in London and the other in Oxford. Apparently the jury shouted 'Hear, hear!' – oh no, they didn't – but he was pardoned by King Charles I who also revoked an order that he be stripped of his university degrees. Gill succeeded his father as high master of St Paul's school but was such an irritable bloke that he ended up back in Oakham where he died in 1643.

Charles Johnson Payne, otherwise known as 'Snaffles', was a painter of hunting scenes who stayed briefly in Oakham before the First World War. His work was renowned for its sense of humour. He also sketched many local characters.

Edward Vere Hodge revitalised Oakham School when he took over as head in 1879. Just as Edward Thring had motivated Uppingham, Hodge was an innovator at Oakham.

Sir John Harington of Exton was credited with inventing the flush toilet in 1597, well ahead of the accredited inventor Thomas Crapper who didn't introduce his famous 'seat of civilisation' until three centuries later. Sir John is remembered among the many fine marble representations of past landowners to be found in Exton church.

Motoring pioneer Frederick Henry Royce linked up with the Hon Charles Rolls in 1904 to lay the basis for the massive aeronautics and engine company. The Ruddle family established the world famous brewery in Langham. The Ellingworths of Oakham not only provided a sequence of town criers but one of the county's finest schoolteachers Dolce Ellingworth. One of her brothers was among the first in Rutland to own a motorcycle.

Suffragette firebrand Mrs Emmeline Pankhurst visited Oakham in June 1907 and, after a typically forceful speech in the market place, was pleased to take high tea afterwards with the Ellingworths.

Other much loved local characters whose names live on in folk lore and memory include Cyril Holmes, the blind seer of Morcott; and 'Fiddler' Brown, a Crimean War hero who was tended by Florence Nightingale at Scutari hospital, and returned to Oakham where he would play his violin to all and sundry with his pet dog at his feet. His funeral in 1910 was said to be one of the biggest ever seen in Oakham.

George Morton, an Oakham builder and strongman, could pick up a steel wheelbarrow with his teeth; and Tiny Thorpe plied his horse coach to and from Manton station in all weathers. These days they would have won some sort of community award.

Baddies included Richard Vicars of Caldecott, a well-known poacher who was still nicking deer well into his 70s; John Perkins, the last person to be hanged in Oakham in 1833, for killing a gamekeeper while poaching in Empingham Woods; and John Smith, who tried to sell his wife and ended up in the stocks. A woman who was also called Smith – but was no relation to John – was flogged for persistent begging. At the time the flogging room was contained in a building in a yard off the High Street.

And so to today when Rutland has so many unsung heroes and heroines to provide an outstanding example to future generations. One is Tommy Suthern, a crackerjack character who, at the time of writing, is in fine fettle at the age of 95.

Tommy's a modest man who would only reluctantly subscribe to his claim to fame as Rutland's last honorary alderman. I called him 'a silver-haired, pocket-sized dynamo' when I interviewed him for the Rutland Times in 1986 and a chance meeting at Oakham library the other week showed he hadn't changed.

A former town mayor of Oakham, chairman of Oakham Urban Council and mainstay of the old Rutland District Council, the former miner and railway trade union official still shops for himself and his son Glyn who runs the menswear shop at Fords department store in Oakham. His other son Keith lives in Solihull.

Tommy can be seen scurrying around town with a shopping bag in hand or planning his next holiday. For years he and Glyn have travelled to watch the Olympic Games and it'll be a poor do if they have to watch it on the telly instead of sitting in the stadium.

Born on Wearside in a poor colliery village, he came down to Rutland when he married his beloved wife Hilda who was from Oakham, on July 9, 1938. The devoted couple were stalwarts at the Salvation Army Citadel for years and Tommy remains a staunch Salvationist. Hilda died, aged 84, but Tommy soldiers on with a twinkle in his eyes and that chirpy north-east accent which has remained defiantly intact after 70 years in Rutland.

As a councillor his philosophy was, 'For the people and for the benefit of the town.'

Aspiring politicians might bear that in mind, for Tom Suthern's assiduous and selfless work in the community has stood him in good stead as an example to us all.

And then there's the equally remarkable Alec Crombie of Uppingham who, though blind since the age of 10, is a much respected solicitor who somehow manages to be an actor – having appeared in many productions with the Uppingham Theatre Company – and tackle marathon walks for blind charities.

One of his treks took him from Wiltshire to Rutland, with a support team helping him to negotiate tricky stiles and other obstacles. Another walk involved every village in Rutland. The fact that he also skis and plays chess to championship standard – in 1986 he took world champion Gary Kasparov to 40 moves in a five-hour match – is equally incredible. "Chess is not a relaxing game but there are no practical difficulties," he says, giving me a demonstration on his modified board.

Alec, 65, was born in Birmingham and is married to Caroline. He carries out his work with a document reader and a scanner with voice software and provides an essential service in the small market town which has been his home for almost exactly 40 years, specialising in wills and estates.

In addition to his talents against the odds, he is totally unsinkable and one of the nicest men in Rutland. Long may his good work continue.

There have been so many fine servants to the Rutland cause over the years. Apart from the aforementioned Eddie Martin, who figureheaded the county's push for independence and who now lives in Cumbria, there is Col James Weir, the first chairman of the council following independence; and Sir Jock Kennedy, a native of Hawick who enjoyed a distinguished RAF career and was a greatly respected Lord Lieutenant for many years.

Col Thomas Haywood of Gunthorpe was Sir Jock's distinguished predecessor as 'Lieutenant responsible for Rutland' during the 'Leicestershire years', and the current Lord-Lieutenant, Dr Laurence Howard of Whissendine, continues to be actively involved in the community.

Roger Begy of Greetham, the most recent council leader, has led county deputations to Westminster on several occasions – usually in pleas for more funding as Rutland competes against larger conurbations for cash. He has also proved a major influence in attracting fresh business to the area and fighting for affordable housing.

Alan Duncan became Tory MP for Rutland and Melton in 1987. An oil trader and adviser on oil supply, shipping and refining, he has since proved invaluable to the county in his support for such campaigns as the retention of Ruddles brewery and the preservation of rural post offices. He is the current Shadow Secretary for Industry.

Amongst the community at large, Bryan Nicholls is a well-known town photographer who was ordained into the Church of England and became vicar of Edith Weston. Malcolm Darby of Preston has written a best-selling book on Yorkshire dialect and plays piano for Uppingham musical revues; John Hackett directs Rutland Musical Theatre productions to the highest standard; Warwick Metcalfe is a cartographic artist of wondrous pedigree who has portrayed Uppingham town centre in detail; and musicians Barry Collett, Albert Cortese and Rodney Dawkins are in constant demand for concerts and lectures.

George Kirk of Langham is another amazing character – a war veteran who proudly wears his RAF uniform to Oakham's Remembrance Day church service, remains a parish councillor and insists that his good health and a sturdy figure are maintained by a tackling a few lengths of the swimming pool each day.

And no review could be complete without mentioning the late Professor Harold Lawton, one of the last survivors of the First World War, who almost died whilst imprisoned in a German PoW camp in 1918 and, 20 years later, was listed in Hitler's 'black book' as being a person to be 'done away with' had the Nazis ever invaded Britain. He was awarded the coveted Legion d'Honneur by the French government and died, a proud centenarian, at Greetham.

There are many more too numerous to mention – though I *will* mention, in passing, the indefatigable Peter Jones of the Oakham Town Partnership, the ebullient Patsy Clifton of teashop fame – a major protagonist for the Oakham bypass; local photographer Jim Harrison, who recently became Mayor of Oakham; Richard Adams, another photographer who is a former town clerk of Oakham and gives some of the finest photographic slide shows I've seen; our own Alan Oliver; esteemed historian Bryan Waites; Joy Gregg, a former Oakham Mayor who was voted The Face of Rutland in a local newspaper poll in 2006; Maureen Dodds of Ranksborough, a Londoner by birth whose heartfelt love of Rutland has been demonstrated many times by her work for the Oakham Carnival, the RATS theatre group and Oakham in Bloom; and fellow 'Bloomer'

Joyce Lucas who, with husband Bob, has been a prime mover in helping OB gain national awards as well as leading an ongoing operation to make the county town a floral credit to its inhabitants. The display of glorious blooms at salient points around Oakham's centre has been enhanced by colourful hanging baskets and the development of the arboretum alongside the county council HQ at Catmose – all very welcome.

To all of you, many thanks.

BIBLIOGRAPHY:

Buxton, Audrey and Brian Martin, *Rutland People – The Genuine Article,* Spiegl Press, Stamford, 2001.

Goldmark, M and A.R. Traylen, *Maps of Rutland: Volume 9,* Spiegl Press, Stamford, 1985.

Hickman, Trevor, *Melton Mowbray to Oakham: Part of the Britain in Old Photographs series,* Sutton Publishing, Stroud, Gloucestershire, 1998.

Hickman, Trevor, *The Best of East Leicestershire & Rutland,* Sutton Publishing, Stroud, Gloucestershire, 2001.

Hill, Raymond, *Burley on the Hill Mansion,* Janet Kirkwood, Witham-on-the-Hill, Bourne, Lincolnshire, 2002.

Palmer, Roy, *Folklore of Leicestershire and Rutland,* Tempus Publishing, Stroud, Gloucestershire, 2002.

Rutland Tourism Authority, *Rutland – A Welcome to England's Smallest County,* Brochure, with photographs by Richard Adams, 1985.

Rutland Tourism, *The Rutland Church Trail – A Guide to 15 Churches,* Brochure produced by Brian Nicholls and Joanne Pagett, 2003.

Sharpling, Paul, *Stained Glass in Rutland Churches,* Rutland Local History and Record Society, Rutland Record Series No 3, 1997.

Spelman, Judith, *Rutland Voices: Part of the Oral History series,* Tempus Publishing, Stroud, Gloucestershire, 2000.

Tew, David, *The Melton to Oakham Canal,* Sycamore Press, Wymondham, 1984.

Traylen, A.R., *Notable Citizens of Rutland – a Compendium of the Famous through to the Infamous from the Records of Time to the mid-20th century,* Spiegl Press, Stamford, 2002.

Trubshaw, Bob, *Little-Known Leicestershire and Rutland,* Heart of Albion Press, Wymeswold, Leicestershire, 1995.

Waites, Bryan, *Rutland Alphabet – a Guide to Rutland's Landscapes and Villagescapes,* Spiegl Press, Stamford, 1985.

Waites, Bryan, *Remember Rutland! – How it is Impossible to Destroy the True English Region,* Spiegl Press, Stamford, 1984.

Waites, Bryan, *Walks in Historic Leicestershire & Rutland,* Countryside Books, Newbury, Berkshire, 2001.

Waites, Bryan, *Uppingham – Photographic Memories,* The Francis Frith Collection, Frith Book Company, Teffont, Salisbury, Wiltshire, 2004.

Waites, Bryan, *Exploring Rutland,* Leicestershire Libraries and Information Service, 1982.

Cottage

Publications

This title is one in a new series by **Cottage Publications**.
For more information and to see our other titles, please visit our website
www.cottage-publications.com
or alternatively you can contact us as follows:–

Telephone: +44 (0)28 9188 8033
Fax: +44 (0)28 9188 8063

Cottage Publications
is an imprint of
Laurel Cottage Ltd.,
15 Ballyhay Road,
Donaghadee, Co. Down,
N. Ireland, BT21 0NG